To Dia ♡,

Press on for our Lord until every tribe on earth has heard --- in their own language.

Blessings

Joe

2 Tim 3:16-17

A POKE IN THE RIBS
BY JACK POPJES

Partners in Bible Translation

Orlando, Florida
1-800-WYCLIFFE • www.wycliffe.org

Visit Wycliffe's website at www.wycliffe.org

A Poke in the Ribs
© 2006 Wycliffe Bible Translators, Inc.
P.O. Box 628200
Orlando, FL 32862-8200

Cover design and layout by Sean Stark. All rights reserved.

ISBN 0-938978-41-1

To order additional copies of *A Poke in the Ribs*, contact Wycliffe's Media Resource Center, 1-800-992-5433, *mrco@wycliffe.org*

CONTENTS

Acknowledgements

At last, the acknowledgement page! The page I have looked forward to writing for so long. For one thing, it is the last page an author writes, which means the work has come to an end at last. For another, it is the page where he can finally lay the blame where it belongs. Whose fault was it this book was published? Many people share the guilt.

A Dutch author of children's books, W. G. van der Hulst, wrote a children's Bible. As a preschooler, I loved that *Kinderbijbel!* Every day I looked at the pictures and listened to the stories. That Dutch storyteller made a deep impact on me. I wanted to tell stories too. He started it, and therefore is blameworthy.

Skip seven years ahead to our first winter in Canada. Every Saturday my dad brought home the weekly newspaper. After reading the comics I searched for the editorial page and read a columnist whose name I can't remember. Nor can I remember anything he wrote. What I do remember is that he wrote about something interesting every week, and that he wrote simply and well, so an immigrant boy could read it. I admired that man. I wanted to do that someday. Yes, this columnist too deserves denunciation.

Then there are people who responded to the emailed columns with these self-incriminating words: "Jack, you need to publish these columns in a book." Annie, Bernie (I'll just use your first names—you know who you are), Chrissy, David (several), Edith, Frank, Garland, Hugh, Ichabod (okay, I made that one up)— Shirley, Philip, Richard... and so on throughout the alphabet. The list is long, their culpability is clear.

One of the D's is Darryl Kernick, who compounded his felony by writing the foreword.

Susan Van Wynen, former vice president of the Communications Department of Wycliffe USA, had the best chance to stop this book from being published. Instead she wrote, "I loved your columns and want to do everything I can to move forward with getting them into a book." She deserves major disapprobation, especially since she got other people involved, like Diane, and a proofreader identified only as F.

The people who read, edited, fixed and critiqued the columns cannot be absolved. I'm sorry to say, even my nearest and dearest are indicted—my wife Josephine, my daughters Valorie and Cheryl, and especially Leanne, who read every column and made the kind of observations (Yuk! Boring! What?! Unclear! No!) that moved me to revise and correct, thus increasing the chances this book would be published.

PREFACE

The grade-nine teacher was preparing her class for a letter-writing exercise. When to write letters, how to, whom to, what, why…on and on she went. I was not listening. While pretending to write in the notebook on my desk, I secretly read a book of stories I held hidden on my lap. "You have forty minutes," the teacher concluded. The class bowed their heads over their papers and, with furrowed brows and bobbing pencils, wrote, erased and wrote again. I kept reading.

Finally, ten minutes before the end of class, I finished my story and closed the book. Then I picked up my pencil and dashed off a letter to an imaginary friend, describing the previous weekend's visit to my uncle's farm. I handed it in with time to spare. Next day the teacher posted it on the class bulletin board as the best letter written.

Just two years before, in 1950, I had immigrated to Alberta, Canada, speaking eight words of English: "Mai naym is Djek, ai kom of Holland." The language-learning process had not been easy. My 12-year-old peers enjoyed creating expressions to describe my inability to understand what was said and speak intelligibly. Of all the names they gave me, "Dummy" is the only publishable one.

All this changed after that letter-writing class. I suddenly enjoyed respect from my schoolmates and my self-esteem grew. (Some say it has never stopped growing.)

I had always been a voracious reader, and from then on wrote prolifically, if not on paper then at least in my head.

Forty years and a Bible translation project later, I found myself in the position of executive director of Wycliffe Canada with a mandate from the board to implement a large number of major changes. The email age had dawned, and my wife advised me to write a weekly email column to keep the worldwide Canadian membership in the information loop. I took her advice and called the columns *The Loop*.

The columns were newsy and very time-oriented, and many were of little lasting interest. But they were successful well beyond helping to make the organizational changes. By the end of six years not only were the 400 Canadian Wycliffe workers reading *The Loop*, they were outnumbered by a growing over-the-shoulder readership from other organizations. I was surprised, and pleased.

The decision to write the next set of weekly email columns as executive director of Wycliffe Caribbean was easy. I called it *The Link*, since I wanted to link together the overseas field workers with the volunteer promotional committees that operated in a dozen sending countries. *The Link* columns differed from the earlier *Loops* in that most of the *Links* had solid material that mentored, taught, oriented, inspired and challenged the readers in the area of cross-cultural missions and Bible translation.

Three years later I started a different column, *The Look*. My focus was on Christian people, worldwide, who ought to be busy evangelizing the world and discipling the nations. A recurring theme is that Bible translation is the most foundational work that any cross-cultural missionary can do.

Readers of these columns have forwarded, copied, republished and even translated them into other languages. They kept asking when they would be available in print form for a wider readership, eventually leading to publishing this book.

The columns the editors and I chose for this book are a tithe. For every column in the book, nine didn't make it. As I chose each column, I asked myself questions about it. Is this column stimulating and possibly entertaining? Will it make people laugh, or at least think? Is it informative and will it help readers understand missions better? Does it challenge readers to make changes in their lives?

Most importantly, will people take the book to school or to business meetings and secretly read it, hiding it on their laps?

The 52 columns in this book are arranged to be read one per week. Betcha can't read just one!

FOREWORD

"If it ain't Dutch, it ain't much"—so the Dutch say, tongue in cheek of course. As a Dutch-born Canadian, Jack Popjes may well add a measure of credibility to the saying, especially when it comes to writing.

I first noted his talent some years ago when he was the director for Wycliffe Caribbean and he began writing his *Link* series of articles. Among them were some real gems. Some touched me personally. Others seemed quite profound. I started filing them away in a folder in my in-box because they were just too good to delete. Then one day I thought, "These ought to be in print," so I wrote to Jack, as others did, and encouraged him to publish his *Link* series so a much wider audience could be inspired by his writings.

Jack is never at a loss for words, but at the same time, he does have a way of finely crafting words. A couple years ago, Wycliffe International established a set of core values. The content was approved but they read oh-so-boring and dull. We sent them to Jack and asked him to breathe life and inspiration into them. The result was amazing and today we have a powerfully expressed statement of core values.

But there is much more to Jack than mere talent with words. Behind the words is a treasury of experience. Walking the journey of Christian faith over many years, much of it lived out among the Canela people of Brazil, where he and his wife Jo worked for 22 years, has honed his perceptions and insights. The result is a remarkable ability to cut through superficiality to touch the true heart of an issue.

This book will not leave you unmoved. It will inspire you. It will challenge you. It will provoke you. Whether through spoken or written word, Jack Popjes leaves you thinking in new ways. This publication is no exception. Jack has given us the "much" even though in reality he "ain't" that Dutch anymore.

Darryl Kernick—Assoc. Exec. Dir., Wycliffe Bible Translators Intl., Inc.

⟶ COLUMN 1 ⟵
A POKE IN THE RIBS

The chapel speaker, passionately describing Bible translation ministry, captured my eyes, my ears and my mind. More than that, I felt a deep, heart-tearing longing for God to use me in a work like that. Oh, to bring a people group the Word of God in their own language! What a life purpose that would be!

Jo and I were taking a summer course of introductory linguistics taught by Wycliffe linguist-missionaries at the University of Washington. "It would be a great life!" I thought. "Not that I don't already have a good life. I do. Life is good. I have it all together." At least I thought so.

I could list many deeply satisfying things. God had given me a beautiful and loving young wife, and our first sweet little girl—plus another one on the way in the fall. I drove a new 1962 Volkswagen Beetle. I was an ordained minister and pastor of a growing church. The Reverend Jack D. Popjes. It sounded good. I enjoyed the prestige of being the youngest board member of my alma mater Bible college. I had all my doctrines and practices in order. Everything I preached and taught was biblically sound. Life was good. I had it all together. But that was before I got a poke in the ribs.

As I listened to that Wycliffe chapel speaker I cried out in my heart, "Oh God, yes! Please, someday, let me be like this missionary. Please use me!"

Suddenly I felt what seemed like someone poking me in the ribs. But the chair next to me was empty. Again I felt that poke and sensed a command to look. Look hard!

I looked, and saw the chapel speaker still speaking with Holy Spirit enthusiasm. Look! Then I saw it. What a shock! The speaker was a woman! A woman teaching me, a man? No, Lord! You can't do that!

Again the command. Look! She was speaking in chapel but wore no hat. Look! She had short hair. Look! She was wearing earrings…and lipstick. Look! The hem of her skirt was above her knees. Look! Oh no, the worst of all. She was not using the King James Authorized Version of the Bible!

In 15 seconds God had smashed six doctrines and practices dear to my church. I, myself, had preached them, and had held each of these opinions equally strongly for years.

That lesson was one of many to beat me into shape—shaping me into a tool God could use. He showed me I did not have it all together. True, some biblical truths were clear and obvious. Jesus is God. He came to die to pay for our sins, and rose again. I am ready to die for these truths and many more like them.

But there are many debatable issues, some mostly cultural, others with a more solid biblical basis. As I learned not to take these debatable issues so seriously, God prepared me to work together with His children—colleagues from scores of denominations, a dozen different countries and a vast array of theological backgrounds. We agreed on the essentials, but held a wide variety of opinions in other areas.

The job of worldwide Bible translation is far too large for any one denomination to accomplish by itself. It is too great for any one country or any one mission agency to achieve. It takes thousands of churches, from every country in the world, working together with hundreds of mission agencies to complete the task of world evangelization, of which Bible translation is such a key component.

Praise God, that is exactly what is beginning to happen in the world right now. There are more ministry partnerships among agencies and churches than ever before in the history of Christianity. More and more each day, Western linguists partner with national translators, and mother-tongue translators work together with foreign missionaries.

Increasingly, denominational differences are seen as being secondary compared to the job of bringing the Word of God to every people group, every language and every subculture on earth. This is good stuff! After all, there are no denominations in heaven, nor any mission agencies.

Jesus prayed earnestly for us Christians just hours before He was nailed to the cross: "Father, I pray…that they may be one as We are…May they be brought to complete unity to let the world know that You sent Me" (John 17:21–23).

God calls all His children, multimillions of them, all around the world, to obey the Great Commission to evangelize the world and disciple the nations.

He may need to poke some of us in the ribs before we humble ourselves and loosen the tight hold we have on our opinions. Then, as we focus on the essentials, He will use us fully to complete the task in this needy world.

Someday God will answer His Son's prayer for unity among us.

Someday all people groups will have His Word in their heart language.

Someday His kingdom will come on earth.

Someday His will shall be done on earth as it is in heaven.

DON'T BOX THEM IN

I don't like being boxed in. I constantly ask myself, What choices do I have? What are my options? No doubt many of you have felt the same way about situations in your life and ministry. I have always valued the opportunity to make a choice and now I know why.

Converted Muslim scholar Lamin Sanneh writes, "Choice and option are essential to being human and responsible. Choice is a prerequisite for personal integrity."[1]

These are strong statements, and biblically true. God gives every human being the power to recognize options, and He is ready to give the wisdom to choose among them. The worst form of manipulation is to take options away from people, and thus force them into one path. No wonder I hate being boxed in!

This became very real to me about 20 years ago, during one of our furloughs in Canada. I habitually accepted every speaking engagement that came my way, speaking two or three times a week. At universities I often had non-Christian audiences and the questions during the question period were always probing and often highly critical of our work.

In that same furlough I took a community college photography course where I learned a highly effective but low technology trick of showing slides. I used two 35 mm slide projectors (remember those?) and two screens set up side by side. I had a remote control in each hand and showed two slides at once as I did a live commentary. Using those techniques, I developed a presentation for potentially critical audiences.

The show started with Canela village scenes showing basic human activities like cooking, eating, mothering, play, work and recreation. This established the fact that the Canela people were not that different from us, even though they met their needs in their own unique way.

Then I mentioned three areas of Canela society that differed greatly from Western society. On the left screen I showed one single slide of an elder talking to a group of young boys. As I summarized the local traditions he was teaching them, my right thumb was busy. On the right screen dozens of images flashed by: schools, libraries, books, computers, classrooms, teachers and universities. I made no comment on these pictures of academia, but simply kept summarizing the old man's explanations of how the world worked.

Then I changed to health and medicine. On one screen, a Canela healer blew smoke on a boy's head. As I described native healing ceremonies, the other screen showed hospitals, operating theatres, pharmacies, doctors, medications, nurses and clinics.

The third area featured a slide of a young woman gazing pensively into the distance. I told of the vague ideas Canelas had about their Creator, the afterlife, and how they feared the ghosts of ancestors and the demons of the forest. Meanwhile, the other screen once again was busy with shots of churches large and small, synagogues, temples of every kind, Bibles, preachers, rabbis, imams, priests, choirs, prayer meetings and study groups.

I concluded by saying, "Our work among the Canela people gives them some options. They can learn to read, or not. They can learn scientific facts about the universe, or not. They can accept modern medicine, or not. They can learn about their loving Creator God, or not. They can choose to believe Jesus died for them, or not. We are giving them the opportunity to choose.

"Each of you sitting here can make choices about God. Some of you have chosen to disbelieve in the God of the Bible. You have that right. But you have no right to deny that choice to the Canelas, or to any other of the hundreds of millions of people in the world who still do not have the Bible in their own language. You have no right to box them in."

The human capacity to choose was built into us by our Creator God. He gave us the right to make choices, and will give us the wisdom to do so, if we ask.

No human being has the right to play God and deny others their basic human right to make choices. Especially choices that will have eternal consequences.

1. Lamin Sanneh, *Whose Religion Is Christianity?: The Gospel Beyond the West* (Grand Rapids, MI: Wm. B. Eerdmans, 2003), 118.

GENTLEMEN, THIS IS A BIBLE

At the risk of being thought of as having a severe case of multiple personality disorder, I need to tell you of the meetings I have with myself. No, I am not an adult survivor of childhood abuse struggling with dissociative conditions. So, you psychiatrists back off; lie down on your own couches. Yet I freely admit I do have meetings with my many selves. Here's why.

Sometimes, in the course of a week's work, I get bogged down. It is not surprising. I sometimes receive and read about 150 email messages a week. I often answer or initiate about 75 a week, sometimes as many as 25 a day. I'm on the phone a lot. I travel…a lot. During three months one fall, I averaged one takeoff and landing every five days. I think, plan and pray. I read my Bible, books and magazines, and check news articles on the Internet. I talk with a lot of people, make a lot of speeches and write articles. Oh yes, and on Friday I write an email column.

Many of you can identify with this kind of lifestyle. And most of you, like me, eventually get bogged down in administrivia. Our thinking slows down. We fret about little things. We start getting behind. We get sidetracked. We feel panic about looming deadlines. We are short with people, even those we love a lot. When that happens to me, I call a meeting with myself.

I circle a dozen chairs around the room. Across the room sit Jack the Grandpa, Jack the Son, Jack the Husband and Jack the Father. To my left sit Jack the Manager, Jack the Listener, Jack the Speaker, Jack the Writer and Jack the Organizer. To my right sit Jack the Chaplain, Jack the Treasurer, Jack the Counselor and Jack the Bible Translator. As needed, I will ask a few more personalities to come in. You get the picture.

I chair the meeting and say, "Thank you all for coming at such short notice." Then I pick up my Bible and hold it for all to see and make the following short speech:

> "Gentlemen, this is a Bible. This Book was written by men and women inspired by the Holy Spirit. It is the Word of God. God reveals Himself to us through this Book. This Book tells us everything we need to know about God's power, wisdom and love. This Book is all about God. Our lives are all about God. Our marriage is about God. Our career is about God. Our lives are not about emails or plane flights, or speeches, or articles. Our lives are all about God.

> "As Christians we all want the message of this Book to be spread to every man, woman and child on earth, and in his or her own language. All of you gentlemen are to a greater or lesser extent involved in making sure that this Book reaches every person on earth in his or her own heart language. But, more importantly, you all need to deepen your intimacy with the God this Book reveals. Because it is all about God. The floor is now open for discussion on how each of you can relate more intimately with Him."

It is interesting to listen to the discussions. Jack the Speaker might say, "Hey, I don't have time for this, I have a message to prepare." Jack the Organizer might say, "But God gave you two full hours tonight, you can do it then." Jack the Chaplain might say, "I will pray that God will clear your mind and help you focus." Sometimes there are loud arguments. Sometimes the discussion gets sidetracked. When it does, I hold up my Bible again.

Back to the basics. God: our Core Value. It's all about Him.

⇒ Column 4 ⇐
In Search of Comfort

Books with the words *In Search of…* in their titles are popular. I found a half a dozen when I googled for those words.

I have often joked that my next book will be called *In Search of Comfort: My Life as a Wycliffe Missionary.* Plenty of evidence proves I searched for ways to provide comfortable places for my family to live, even under the most rigorous conditions. A house with mud walls, earth floor and a palm-leaf roof can be made comfy. Numerous trees bearing scars from hammock ropes are a mute testimony to the fact that I learned to find comfort where it could be found. I always found ways for my family and work associates to sit softer, preferably in the shade, and with plenty of privacy. Not that we often got it, but I was searching, searching for comfort.

I am not, however, going to write *In Search of Comfort.* My potential readership in the developed nations is already very good at searching for and finding comfort.

One evening, after returning to Canada from a long period of travel, I sat back and watched TV for the first time in six months. The furniture advertising jumped out at me: "Come on, get more comfortable. You deserve the best." Nonsense! A life of extreme self-love, sitting in the centre of our comfort zone, is not what we as Christians are called to live.

The book I would like to write is one called *In Search of Power.* Not human but divine, Holy Spirit power. This kind of power leads to significant achievement, getting things done. You will not find it in your comfort zone, but in the risk zone. I once had a colleague who, when faced with making a tough decision, was fond of saying, "I'm not sure I am comfortable with this option." This made me see red faster than anything else. I used to feel like jumping up and shouting angrily, "It is not about being comfortable! It's about getting something done! It's about moving things ahead!"

I doubt Abram was comfortable with leaving his home and trekking north to a land he knew nothing about. Later he stepped further into the risk zone when, knife in hand, he was about to cut the throat of his only son.

Moses enjoyed a good, comfortable living, and stated repeatedly that he was not comfortable with the idea of confronting Pharaoh, but he moved into the risk zone anyway.

Gideon was not comfortable with sending all but 300 soldiers home, but he risked it.

Esther risked instant execution when she walked into the king's presence without being invited, but she did it anyway.

The fisherman-disciples had to leave the comforts of a secure, profitable fishing business to wander about the countryside with an itinerant preacher. Later they risked their lives to carry out Jesus' commands.

Each one of the heroes of Scripture, at one time or another, stepped out of his or her comfort zone into the zone of risk and there found the power to work miracles.

God has ordered His Church to go out, evangelize the world and disciple the nations. This won't get done if we choose only what we are comfortable doing.

Our search for power to accomplish this worldwide vision will take us into the risk zone. But we don't need to fear; God is with us in the risk zone.

Running risks together with God—that's not a bad option. I can be comfortable with that.

⊹ COLUMN 5 ⊹
ENTERING CODGERHOOD

Life is measured by milestones: our first day in Grade 1, our first driver's license, our first paying job, falling in love for the first time. This week marked a milestone for me: I received my first Old Age Security check. (Never mind the congratulations and smart remarks!)

Now that I am officially a codger [codg·er *n. Informal.* A somewhat eccentric man, especially an old one] I took time to ponder this newly acquired status. Terms like *senility, decrepitude* and *dotage* spring to mind. But I have a hard time applying them to myself. After all, there is nothing wrong with being old. I'd rather have old, secondhand diamonds than not have any at all.

So what is it like to be a codger? The old saying, "You are only as old as you feel," is no help at all. Sometimes I feel like a 22-year-old rebel, setting out to change the world, but a few days ago, after lifting and carrying boxes during a cleanup day, I felt like a 98-year-old ready to pass from the scene. But I seem to have reached that stage when people look old who are only my age.

I am discovering that old age is like a bank account. You withdraw from it only what you have already put in. I am now withdrawing back and shoulder pains from the deposit of my first job in the oil business, which was mostly lifting and carrying heavy steel pipes. On the other hand, I am also withdrawing much deep-down satisfaction knowing the Canela people of Brazil have the Word of God in their own language because of our family's work there. And I withdraw tons of pleasure from our children and grandchildren. Children are certainly a great comfort in my old age, although without them I wouldn't have reached it as fast.

The main problem with old age is that there is not much future in it. Yet I do feel it is all a matter of perspective. If, for instance, there were

15 months in every year instead of 12, I would be only 48. Hey, that's not old! Besides, I don't consider myself truly old until the candles on the birthday cake cost more than the cake, and lighting them sets off the smoke alarm.

Passing this milestone equalizes life. For instance, as a young man I aspired to things that never came to pass, but I am making up for it now, since as an old man I remember things that never happened.

And I still have aspirations. I still want to do things that will live on after me, things that will be useful for others. Possibly a well-developed and updated Canela-Portuguese dictionary for Canelas, missionaries and researchers to use. And a book or two that will bring pleasure and insight to my grandkids and their friends. I want to plant trees in whose shade I know I will never sit.

I am still enthusiastic about Bible translation. No, not to do it myself, but to talk, write, promote and do whatever I can to help people get involved. May I never outlive my enthusiasm.

I'm also ready for any surprises God may be holding behind His back. After all, He promised that "the righteous will flourish like a palm tree…they will still bear fruit in old age, they will stay fresh and green, proclaiming, 'The Lord is upright; he is my Rock'" (Ps. 92:12–15).

I wonder what He has in mind for me? I can hardly wait!

⟶ COLUMN 6 ⟵
WHO TEACHES WHOM?

One weekend as I was reading a couple of books on theology, I found myself feeling increasingly irritated. One of the books was a collection of current essays on aspects of today's Christianity written by a number of different authors. After reading several articles carefully, and scanning most of the rest, I felt exasperated.

No, it wasn't that I didn't agree with many of the concepts explained and problems explored by the writers. And it certainly wasn't because the theologians were not well-educated. The string of academic degrees behind each of their names was impressive. So was the list of prestigious educational institutions they attended and outstanding ministries in which they served.

Then it hit me. Although each one talked about "the Church" and "current Christianity," discussing situations and problems among evangelical believers, they were North American theologians talking to Americans about the Church in North America only. I went through the book again. Sure enough, none of the writers had served in cross-cultural ministries outside of North America. Not one of them mentioned the Church in Africa, Asia and South America. Not even once! Yet they wrote as if they were talking about Christ's whole Church on earth.

Whoa! Wait a minute! At least 70 percent of Christ's Church is located outside of North America and Europe. The Church worldwide grew 1100 percent during the 1900s. Currently 30,000 people become Christians every day, but not in the Western, developed nations. Well over 40,000 non-American, non-Western national missionaries are involved in career missions around the world.[1]

I have no problem with American theologians writing to Americans about the American church today. But I do have a problem with them writing as if the Church in America is "the whole Church." Hey, some of the problems they wrote about don't even exist outside of North America. (Yale professor Lamin Sanneh's book, *Whose Religion Is Christianity?: The Gospel Beyond the West*, stands in stark contrast to those theological books I was reading.)[2]

It is high time for those highly educated American theologians to learn not only *about* the Church in the rest of the world, but to learn *from* the non-Western Church.

I once spoke with an evangelical bishop from China and asked him if we Western Christians had anything to teach the 70 million believers in China. He replied, "Oh, yes. We Chinese need much teaching in the Word and training in many aspects of ministry. But before you Western missionaries can teach our Chinese believers, you will need to develop a theology of suffering." Then he astounded me with the fact that each one of the pastors in the large group he led had spent an average of 17 years in Chinese prisons. Now there is a learning experience!

The North American church has much to offer the rest of the world. Hundreds of millions of people still do not have even one verse of Scripture translated in their own language. We have money and expertise and can help in training, as well as in hands-on ministry.

But when we come, we need to do so in humility. They outnumber us two to one. They daily practice the kind of Christianity we rarely experience. They have suffered in ways we cannot imagine. We need to come as learners, teachers and partners.

1. *The Church Around the World; Lost People; Poverty,* videos (Madison, WI: InterVarsity/Urbana, 2000).

2. Lamin Sanneh, *Whose Religion is Christianity?: The Gospel Beyond the West* (Grand Rapids, MI: Wm B. Eerdmans, 2003).

→ Column 7 ←
But Because I Love You

Valentine's Day, a day for lovers, is observed in many parts of the Western world. Hundreds of thousands of Valentine's cards are exchanged by husbands and wives, and by boyfriends and girlfriends. On the Sunday closest to February 14, thousands of preachers will seize the opportunity to speak of God's love, very likely using Paul's love poem in 1 Corinthians 13 as their text.

And rightly so. God, after all, is love. He is the living embodiment of every line of that great Love Chapter. I remember memorizing it in the Shakespearian language of the King James Authorized Version: "Charity suffereth long, and is kind; charity envieth not; charity vaunteth not itself, is not puffed up." Today people read it from a modern version such as the New International Version: "Love is patient, love is kind."

But who cares in what version we read it or memorize it? What matters is, having understood it, how we implement the truth of these lovely words with the people we encounter every day. We do this by recognizing that love is a choice.

Choosing to love our spouse, child, friend, or even our enemy means more than mouthing those three words: "I love you." When we say "I love you" to someone, God, according to Paul's poem, wants us to mean this:

- You may at times exasperate me, but because I love you, I will choose to be patient with you.

- You may at times treat me badly, but because I love you, I will be kind to you.

- You may be much superior to me in many ways, but because I love you, I will not envy you.

- I may be superior to you in some ways, but because I love you, I will not brag about myself to you, nor be proud of who I am or of what I have done.

- You may at times be rude to me, but because I love you, I will not be rude to you.

- You may at times be headstrong and opinionated, but because I love you, I will never manipulate you to get my own way.

- You may at times do or say things I don't like, but because I love you, I will not respond in anger.

- You may at times do things to hurt me or wrong me in some way, but because I love you, I will forgive you and not keep track of them.

- You may at times make life hard for me, but because I love you, I will always persevere in deepening our relationship.

- Because I love you, I will always support you, always trust you and always expect the best of you, giving you the benefit of any doubt.

- You might let me down, but because I love you, I will never fail you.

This is exactly how God loves us. Obviously His standard goes far beyond human love. Yet this is the way God wants to love others through us. And not just the people we know personally right around us.

This is also the way He loves hundreds of millions of people who do not yet know Him. God wants us to deliver His Valentine's card, the Bible, to all the people groups who still do not have it in their own language.

→ COLUMN 8 ←
BE MY VALENTINE - RSVP

Forty-four years ago, I made a choice that potentially left millions of people disappointed, or perhaps relieved. I asked Jo to marry me, and she accepted the invitation. I committed myself to her, gave her my name and all that I owned, or would own in the future. I committed to love and protect her. We married not only for better or for worse: we married for good.

Every day I set myself to love Jo and she sets herself to love me. Sometimes we make it easy for each other to do this, sometimes we make it hard, but we do it, which is why we are still married. She is still glad I proposed and I am still glad she accepted.

Fifty-three years ago, I was on the receiving end of a similar invitation. God invited me to become His son, and I accepted His astonishing invitation. He committed Himself to me, gave me His Name and all that He owned. He committed to love and protect me. We began a love relationship that has had its rough spots—not His fault—but which continues to grow.

Both of these relationships started with an invitation, an invitation with an RSVP: Please Respond.

Even though God is Master of the universe, and it is all about Him, He chose to include human beings in His cosmic plans.

God limits Himself in a number of ways. He limited Himself to the weaknesses of a human body when He lived on this planet for 33 years. He limits Himself, at least to a great extent, to operate in this world mostly in response to the prayers of His people. He limits Himself to evangelize the world through the work of His Spirit-filled Church. And, when He invites people into a relationship with Himself, He limits Himself to accepting those who respond to His invitation.

Christians, therefore, are in the most enviable situation on earth.

God is our Lover. He called us, and we responded. Now He treats us as a loving husband would treat his wife on Valentine's Day. I confess, I do not know why He loves us. I know some of you and I have no idea why God loves you. (Juuust kidding!) But I am not kidding when I say I don't know why He loves me.

God does not need me, or you or any of us. I chalk it up to yet another mystery that God may, or may not, reveal to us someday. We just are not smart enough to understand why God does some things. He is omniscient, knowing everything; we are "nonscient," knowing nothing. (As a linguist, I am allowed to make up words.)

On Valentine's Day Jo and I, just as many other husbands and wives, celebrate our love relationship. I love her, she loves me. In the same way, we can celebrate our love relationship with our Heavenly Lover. He loves us, and we love Him.

Human lovers find creative ways to show their love for each other. So does God. He finds millions of creative ways to show His love for us. Sometimes it is a particularly beautiful sunset, or an extra good night's sleep. Sometimes it is a difficult day during which He helps us to grow stronger. Sometimes it is weakness or fear or despair that forces us to turn to Him for strength, love and peace. Sometimes it is…(fill in your own experience of God's love).

Now it is our turn. May we, not only on Valentine's Day, but every day, find creative ways to show our love to both our in-house lover and our Heavenly Lover. We love Him because He first loved us (1 John 4:19). He started it, we responded.

One of the best ways to show our love to our Heavenly Lover is to be involved in translating His "Be My Valentine" invitation into the languages of all the people in the world.

How can people accept God's astonishing invitation unless they can read it in their own language?

THE MISSIONARIES WHO STOLE THE VILLAGERS' HEALTH

The Canela people of Brazil were sickly and weak when we first came to live and work with them. Although our family also caught some of the diseases common in the village, we, in contrast, were pretty healthy. One day an old man looked at me and made what I thought was a joke.

"You are all so healthy; no wonder so many of us are so sick," he said. Years later I realized he had not been joking, but was expressing an important concept from the Canela worldview.

The way people see the world affects the way they think, speak, and live. Unfortunately, the worldviews held by thousands of societies and cultures are based on traditions, few of which have a scientific basis. What's more, most of them do not reflect biblical truth. Thus, many individuals and societies are driven by false concepts.

Traditionally the Canela people, like many other societies, had a worldview that included the concept of "the limited good."[1] They viewed their world as a box—a closed system. In this box were limited amounts of wealth, good luck and health, etc. Since there was only a limited amount of health to go around, and my healthy family obviously had more than our share, the old man believed that somehow we had taken good health away from those Canelas who were now sick.

Canelas who worked hard in their fields, planting much and thus reaping much, were not praised for their hard work, but criticized for having so much. It was felt they must somehow have gotten richer at the expense of others who did not have as much—even though these others may not have worked as hard. The only way a Canela person could be rich and not be criticized was to travel outside of the cultural area and bring goods or money from the city. They saw this as enriching the whole Canela village.

We tend to expect traditional, indigenous societies like the Canelas to have faulty worldviews. Even world leaders, however, seem to operate under this idea of the limited good.

As soon as people and governments started giving donations to help out in the 2004 Sumatra tsunami disaster, world leaders began to express concern about the continuing humanitarian disaster in Africa. UN Secretary-General Kofi Annan pleaded with donors not to shift donations from other projects, but to find extra money to donate to the tsunami calamity.

These world leaders were driven by a legitimate fear that the strong focus by the world media on the suffering caused by the tsunami would make it easy for people to forget about other needs. But some of their fear was also driven by their unbiblical worldview: "There is only so much money in the world, and only a limited amount is available for disaster relief." Not so. Some months later, it appeared that there was plenty of funding for all the projects.

Unfortunately, secular world leaders are not the only ones who operate on the unbiblical worldview. Christians do too, and, yes, even missionaries!

When I served in a leadership position in Wycliffe Canada, we began a fund-raising program, sending out letters presenting field projects for funding. We sent these letters to the personal financial partners of our Wycliffe workers. The first letter was to give these partners the opportunity to opt out of receiving the fund-raising letters. Some did, most did not.

Within months of starting these fund-raising mailings, I began to get notes from some of our workers overseas who were concerned that their financial partners would divert their gifts from their ministries, and give to the projects.

Except in a few cases, the opposite was true. Many financial partners did give to the projects. Then they not only continued to give to the field ministries they supported—in many cases, they increased the amount. This happened in instance after instance. My wife and I experienced it ourselves. Our missionaries were reminded that God is rich, not only in grace but in money.

The Bible's teaching about wealth, money and goods is that people can create wealth. It also teaches that God is involved, and that, therefore, there are no limits. The world is not a box—a closed-in system. Our worldview needs to include our limitless God. He blows the lids off our boxes and kicks out the sides. And that is not a joke.

All good things flow from our Creator God and belong to Him. The supply is limitless.

1. George Foster, "Peasant Society and the Image of Limited Good," *American Anthropologist* 67 (April 1965).

Who Needs TV When You Have Lizards?

While having dinner with our children and grandkids, I remembered our evening meals in Brazil where our daughters grew up. We would watch as moths, attracted by the lights, gathered against the outside of the dining room window screens. The lizards would provide great entertainment as they stalked and grabbed the fluttering insects. Two lizards, going for the same prey, generated the same excited cheering as a soccer game. Afterward we watched the process of the lizard swallowing the moth, and counted, through the translucent skin of his belly, how many he had already eaten.

It got me thinking of some of the little-known blessings of being a missionary and raising a family on the mission field. Sometimes the folks in sending churches back home feel sorry for the children of career missionaries who "sacrifice so much" when going to the mission field. They may be right. On the other hand, they just may not understand. For instance, where's the sacrifice in watching lizards instead of TV? And what about the following benefits culled from the lives of our own three girls who grew up in Brazil?

- They have friends in, or from, a dozen different countries.

- Their pictures decorate the doors of a hundred refrigerators.

- They know what *real* coffee tastes like.

- They know how to create their own entertainment.

- They know that the only things they really need to travel are tickets, passport and money.

- They know as much about dysentery, intestinal parasites and tropical ulcers as most doctors back home—just from participating in dinner table conversations.

- They know how to pack, and pack fast.

- They can speak at least one language other than their own.

- They had adventures kids back home can't even dream of.

- Adults pay them to teach them English.

- They have experienced reality by seeing children they played with and adults they knew die, and by helping to bury them the same day.

- They have scores of uncles, aunts, grandmas and grandpas who are not related to them.

- They know that cultures differ from each other, and that all of them have both good and bad aspects.

- They have never met a food they didn't like—eventually.

There are, of course, some things many missionary kids don't know, or don't do. For example:

- Although they fluently speak two or three languages, they can't spell in any of them.

- Although they know and discuss the relative merits of various international airlines, they can't tell a Ford from a Chevy.

- Although they have had a passport since they were 6 years old, at age 18 they still do not have a driver's license.

- Although they have lived under many types of government, they are not convinced that democracy is the only viable form of government.

- Although they know how to sleep well on the floor, or in a hammock, they don't always dream in their own language.

- Although they can pick up a pencil from the floor with their bare toes, they can't find a store that has shoes to fit their extra wide size.

- Although they always know what they need, they don't always know what they want.

- Although they have been home in college for a year, they can't seem to break the habit of banging their shoes together and shaking them upside down before putting them on.

- Although they have lived in many cities and countries, they don't know how to answer the question, "Where are you from?"

St. Paul, the missionary, with lizards but without TV, said, "I have learned to be content whatever the circumstances" (Phil. 4:11).

SEABISCUIT AND HOMO SAPIENS

I watched a movie recently, the true story of an abused and neglected racehorse named Seabiscuit that eventually became a legendary American racehorse. I came away with a better understanding, not just of what a jockey and a trainer can do with a messed-up horse, but what God has done for the messed-up human race. In addition, I am more convinced than ever of the need for cross-cultural missions and Bible translation.

We human beings are called Homo sapiens: *Homo,* meaning man, and *sapiens,* meaning wise. We are the wise or thinking man. The being that can think, reason, deduce, analyze and come to conclusions, and thus guide his future behaviour wisely. God, who created Homo sapiens, intended for us to live thoughtful lives. But, like the horse Seabiscuit, we have forgotten what we are supposed to be. We tend to act and to live thoughtlessly, simply reacting, as if by instinct, to whatever stimulus Satan sends our way. Our daily newspapers and nightly TV news reports give evidence of the problems and disasters thoughtless humanity generates every day.

God wants people to think biblically, to reason and act believing in the truth of what He has said in His Word. Satan, on the other hand, does not want people to respond with wholesome thoughts. He provokes them to animal-like, knee-jerk, often selfish reactions without a thought of God in their minds. It is scary how Satan keeps people from thinking. I know people who cannot stand silence. They turn on the radio or the TV first thing in the morning and leave it on all day. Their minds are constantly distracted from focused thought. They become addicted to mental noise, afraid even of physical silence. One person told me about a power failure in her home causing the TV to be off for most of the day: "It felt as if someone close to me had died," she said.

Not even Christians are immune to Satan's pressures to keep us from thinking biblically. Some of us have automatic "pat answers" to problems and doubts; others accept political agendas unthinkingly; others are addicted to entertainment, even in church services; others need the constant distraction of people around them. Many people put thinking on the back burner and base their life decisions on feelings. Preachers in some churches tend to avoid thoughtful analysis and application of Scripture, depending on emotion alone to motivate people. All of us are influenced by visual media that keeps shortening our attention span. We need to wake up to this battle for our minds.

The abused horse Seabiscuit had forgotten he was a racehorse and had to learn to be a racehorse again. We human beings, abused by Satan, have forgotten that we are Homo sapiens. We have to learn to be thinking, wise men and women again.

This is not easy. We can't relearn to think on our own any more than Seabiscuit could relearn to be a racehorse on his own. He needed a wise trainer and a patient, determined jockey to redeem or salvage him. He needed to be released from the confinement of the barn, the ropes and the fences to run in the open countryside. Humanity too needs a Redeemer. Praise God, we have Jesus who came to salvage the human race. He releases us from our addiction to din, distraction and dependence on feelings alone, to turn us once again into men and women who think biblically about everything in their lives.

"The fear of [or respect for] the Lord is the beginning of wisdom" (Ps. 111:10). True Homo sapiens believe God exists and give Him the respect He deserves. They do so by including Him in all their thoughts. Just as the most desperately messed-up individuals can be redeemed and transformed through the Word of God, so the most dysfunctional cultures, societies and nations can be redeemed and transformed into what God intended for them to be. But they cannot be redeemed without the Word of God in the language of the people.

That is why cross-cultural missions and Bible translation are so absolutely essential. Through the Bible in the language of the people, whole nations can be redeemed and discipled, their people learning again how to be Homo sapiens: wise, thinking men and women.

Someday we will see and experience redeemed people from all people groups worshiping God in heaven—doing what they were created for with all their hearts and souls and minds.

That's even better than a good movie.

COST AND RISK

Life on planet Earth is full of risks. Some time ago, two sets of seven people died in North America because they took a risk. Early in the morning, before the television cameras of the world, seven astronaut-scientists in the space shuttle *Columbia* died in flames as their craft disintegrated on reentry. Later that same day, in a lonely valley 3,000 kilometres north of where that tragic event took place, seven high school youths died in an avalanche of snow and ice in the Rocky Mountains. The second tragedy struck close to home. The Wycliffe Canada office is located in Calgary, the home of those young people. We can see those Rockies from our office.

What makes highly trained astronauts and young backcountry skiers risk such life-endangering hazards? There is only one answer: the rewards.

The astronauts faced the perils associated with their job, but accepted them for scientific achievement and the unique thrill of being involved in a major human accomplishment, as well as to garner some personal fame. The 15-year-old skiers also risked the threat of a potential avalanche for rewards. Trekking through the cold and snow, far from civilization, gives plenty of opportunity to build character and self-knowledge. The thrill of skiing down sunny slopes and the adventure of the trip, no doubt, also motivated them.

Neither the astronauts nor the skiers were foolhardy. The astronauts were part of a gigantic network of skilled people, costly machinery and advanced technology all focused on bringing them back safely. The kids, too, were well led by experienced leaders, following a well-planned program. They knew the menace of sudden avalanches bearing down upon them. They had done their homework. All packed shovels to help dig themselves and others out. All had electronic locator devices strapped close to their bodies. Both the astronauts and the skiers had paid the price of preparation. They were not presumptuous, but took the risk, and died.

As we watched the skiers' funerals on TV, and listened to interviews with Canadian astronauts, we were struck with the attitudes of the people left behind.

"We will learn from what happened, but the school will continue to make rigorous outdoor activities such as backcountry skiing a part of the curriculum," said a spokesperson for the high school.

"I'm not an astronaut because it's safe," Canadian astronaut Chris Hadfield said, "but...it is worth the risk."

How does this apply to Wycliffe and other agencies focused on cross-cultural missions? There is a guaranteed cost to preparing to get this job done. Churches pay a price when they assign some of their best people, gifted teachers and skilled volunteers to work in Bible translation.

Financial partners too pay a price when they invest ever larger amounts of money to fund the Bible translation ministry.

The individuals getting involved in cross-cultural missions also face costs as they prepare for ministry. They pay the price of loneliness, discouragement and culture stress.

Missions organizations such as Wycliffe spend much time and money preparing workers for the tasks ahead.

Yet even after the costly price of preparation has been paid, risks remain. The workers know they risk disease, loss of property, even death on the field. But they press on in faith, believing that God is ultimately in charge, and that He is with them everywhere they go.

Churches and individual financial partners also face risks. Will all the labour and expense of translating the Bible eventually result in transformed lives and renewed societies? How long will this take? This too takes faith in God.

Life on planet Earth is increasingly full of risks, but we can't live our lives avoiding them all. Whether it is exploring space or skiing the backcountry valleys, it is impossible to achieve a worthwhile accomplishment without paying the cost of preparation and then running the risk of failure and disaster.

The greater the achievement you want, the greater the risk you must take.

This maxim certainly fits worldwide Bible translation. Reaching the last 2,500 people groups with God's Word in their own language—what better reward for which to risk our lives?

The Ultimate Palm Sunday

On Palm Sunday a billion Christians remember and celebrate the triumphal entry of Jesus, the Prince of Peace, into Jerusalem about 2,000 years ago. People waved palm branches and cheered Him as the One to bring peace to their troubled nation. During Palm Sunday liturgies, I often remember a similar scene from my childhood in Holland.

I squirmed and squeezed my thin seven-year-old body through the jostling crowd until I conquered a spot on the curb. The bright sunshine warmed my face, arms and bare knees as I squinted into the light. I clutched my little paper flag, the Dutch red, white and blue, ready to wave, ready to shout and ready to sing a welcome to our rescuers. It was Tuesday, May 8, 1945.

The approaching rumble of a column of Canadian army trucks started the crowd up the road cheering and singing. The noise grew louder until huge dull green trucks blocked out the sun. Shouting, laughing soldiers waved their machine guns from the backs of the trucks. The applause and cheers of the delirious crowd lining the street drowned out the singing of *Wilhelmus*, the Dutch national anthem.

Young soldiers whistled at the tall blonde girl jumping up and down behind me. Her homemade rose petal perfume fought the stink of the diesel exhaust fumes and the stench of close-pressed sweating bodies—bodies and clothing that had not been touched by soap for years.

Camouflaged tanks grumbled past, pulling long-snouted artillery. Their thunderous booming had kept me awake for several nights. Now the cannons were sniffing the air, eager to rout the enemy from the next city.

The cheers died down suddenly as a column of prisoners of war in grey-green uniforms shuffled past. The Luger pistol holsters flapped empty on their brown leather belts. They held their now-empty hands high, or fingers laced on top of their heads. Canadian soldiers, each with his machine gun at the ready, walked alongside them.

The crowd stood silently watching the infantry prisoners go by, but then began to boo and hiss as a small column of Gestapo officers came into view. Finally! No more strutting. No more haughty looks. No more death-dealing commands. Their once-feared black uniforms glistened with the slime of saliva as people rushed from the sidewalk to spit on them.

The last truck in the parade rolled past. I cheered myself hoarse, and waved my little flag until a soldier snatched it out of my hand and waved it high as his truck rumbled on down the road. I tasted the salt of tears, not for the loss of the flag, but for the joy of knowing the peace-bringers had arrived and the enemy would never make me afraid again.

On Palm Sunday I not only think of that event out of my childhood, but my mind also shoots ahead, to the world's very last Palm Sunday. St. John described the celebrants in Revelation 7. "They were wearing white robes and were holding palm branches in their hands." They were waving palm branches, cheering Jesus, the Lamb, at the centre of the heavenly throne. "Salvation belongs to our God, who sits on the throne, and to the Lamb!"

What thrills me the most, however, is the identity of these ecstatic crowds on that ultimate Palm Sunday—uncountable billions of people from all over the world, "from every nation, tribe, people and language."

Thousands of people groups, however, still live in territory occupied by the enemy. They too need to be rescued by the Prince of Peace. They too need to hear God's Good Liberation News in their own language. When they do, they too will join us in celebrating the ultimate Palm Sunday.

⁑ COLUMN 14 ⁂
THAT FIERCE JOY

In my Good Friday readings from the four Gospels, two things struck me that have a strong bearing on the Bible translation missions task and its part in evangelizing the world and discipling the nations.

Firstly, I was struck again by the torment our Lord suffered as He died for us. I read the description of the brutal beatings, the skin-ripping whipping, and the six-hour-long agony of struggling for every breath, as He died nailed to the cross. I cannot imagine what that would be like. I have never, ever, even remotely suffered anything like that. I don't know personally anyone who has.

Secondly, I was struck by Christ's joy-driven, steadfast resolution to endure to the end. "Jesus resolutely set out for Jerusalem," Luke tells us in 9:51, when He left Galilee for the last time. "For the joy set before Him, [He] endured the cross" (Hebrews 12:2). Jesus knew He would pay a terrible price for going through with God's plan of redemption, yet He was driven to pay that price by a fierce joy.

Ah! Now, that part I understand! That intense, ardent joy was the same joy that for over 20 years pulled my wife and me through all kinds of grief and pain to complete the Canela translation program.

I vividly remember one incident—yet another vehicle breakdown on the way into the Canela village in Brazil. It was early afternoon, the hottest part of the day. As I slid underneath the truck with my tools, the sand burned my sweating bare back, hot oil blistered my chest, horseflies bit my bare legs. What little wind there was blew fine sand into my eyes. Hot metal motor parts singed my fingers and forearms as I struggled to fix the problem. Not enjoyable.

Yet, as I crawled out from under that truck, put the tools away and wiped the grease off my hands, I remember muttering to myself with a fierce joy, "Someday...someday they *will* have God's Word. It *will* be worth it all!" And, ten years later, they *did* receive the Word, and it *was* worth it! My eyes sting with tears as I relive this incident and write this paragraph.

It was this same fierce, ardent and intense joy that motivated Jesus to pay the ultimate price, thus opening the way to God for all mankind.

This same joyful vision—thousands of people groups understanding God's message of love for the first time, and turning to Him—drives Wycliffe workers and other cross-cultural missionaries.

The vision of uncounted millions of people from every ethnic group, every language and every nation, worshiping God before His throne in heaven, keeps millions of people on their knees, joyfully praying for His kingdom to come.

The deep-down joy of bringing glory to God through total world evangelization moves Christians from every denomination to pour multimillions of dollars into foreign missions and Bible translation every year.

We know the promise of glory ahead. We see the end result by faith. We know God is at work moving the hearts of people to go, to give, to pray, to turn to Him. We glory in this, and exult with joy unspeakable.

Charles Wesley sang of this too:

> Faith, mighty faith, the promise sees, and looks to God alone;
> Laughs at impossibilities, and cries, "It shall be done!"

Yes, it shall! And this Easter I will celebrate the Great Victory with God's people more joyfully than usual.

+ COLUMN 15 +
MARRY THE RIGHT WOMAN

The celebration of 80 years of marriage doesn't come around every year.

Okay, before you do the math and conclude Jo and I must have Noah's life span, let me explain: I am counting 40 years for me, and 40 years for my wife. That represents a lot of wedded bliss—at least four or five years. Juuust kidding!

For years I had a poster in my office that listed all the things a person should do to succeed in life. The first recommendation was, "Marry the right person." That is exactly what I did when God brought her into my life. Jo was the perfect person for me when I proposed to her nearly 41 years ago in a youth camp on an Alberta lakeshore. She knew that God would help her deal with an overbearing, egocentric Dutchman.

She has been the wife I need ever since. Without her, I may never have joined Wycliffe Bible Translators and gone to live in the rain forests of Brazil. Nor would we have completed a translation program. I was heading for Europe to do mass evangelism. Yet Wycliffe turned out to be a good match. "Wycliffe needs a rebel like you to shake things up," someone once told me by way of encouragement.

Jo went through a lot because of me. Not just three pregnancies during our poverty-stricken days as a bi-vocational pastor of a small church, but also the embarrassment of joining Wycliffe under probation. During our missionary training, I tended to handle culture stress through humour laced with sarcasm. No trainer likes a big-mouthed rookie to put him down. Not even if the joker is a Dutchman.

In the early years of marriage, I took Jo for granted. Not only that,

I spent inappropriate amounts of time with other people. My neglect caused her deep emotional stress, yet she kept on loving me. Later on I tended to be work-driven, leaving little energy for my family. She made me take the time for our girls, and both they and I are grateful. Many years later, when the government shut down our translation work for several years, I was deeply depressed, but she stood by me until the Lord restored my insight and vision.

She has been a great mom, and now is a tremendous grandma. Even so, when the call came to leave house and home, children and grandchildren, she was ready to come with me to work in a new overseas assignment. Mind you, the destination was not totally unpleasant. The Caribbean has beaches and Jo does like the beach!

During these 40 years she has been a fantastic helper to me. The Canela translation project would never have been completed without Jo. With my creative abilities and fluency in the language, and her gift for critiquing my translation work, we produced a good Bible translation. She has always been the people- and relationships-oriented person on the team, while I am the task-oriented pusher—an effective combination.

I remember as a boy celebrating my grandparents' fortieth wedding anniversary. My Frisian grandparents, Pake and Beppe, sat underneath a banner that proclaimed, "40 Jier Hecht Aaniensmeid." (40 Years Solidly Smithed Together.) As a blacksmith heats two pieces of iron, and hammers them until they form one piece, so God, the heavenly Blacksmith, has used the fires of adversity and the repeated blows of His hammer to forge Jo and me into one. That has been our experience. To be made one like that has been our goal. That is what we want for all God's people: to marry the right person (if they are going to marry) and, no matter what it takes, be joined into one by our Blacksmith.

THE EASTER CONFUSION CONTINUES

"Somebody probably tried to stab him and he held up his hands. That's how he got holes right through his palms. Yes, I am sure he was killed in a fight."

"No, I heard he was executed. But they didn't club him on the head to kill him, the way we would, they nailed him to a pole and left him to die."

"Yeah, I heard they killed a couple of thieves at the same time."

Suddenly it dawned on me that the Canela village elders were arguing about the death of Jesus. I was sitting on the hard-packed red clay of the village central plaza, as I usually did in the late afternoon. From a respectful distance, I strained to hear what the elders' council was saying. I was always hoping to hear a new word or expression to jot down in the little notebook. Now I listened even more closely and prayed silently for an opportunity to explain.

Abruptly the chief held up his hand, stopping the argument. "Wait," he said. He pointed at me with his lips and said, "There's our nephew Prejaka. He has been among the Brazilians in town. He probably knows why they treat this week so special."

Moments later I sat down among the elders. As they crowded closer I said, "When, long ago, God was on earth, His name was Jesus. He had 12 followers who later wrote down the things He said and did and what happened to Him in the end."

The chief interrupted, "Wouldn't it be good if we had those notebooks! We could just read about it for ourselves."

The elders shook their heads. "But that was long ago, and those notebooks are all lost and gone. Besides, they would be in some language we don't understand."

I breathed a prayer of thanks and said, "Actually, those books did not get lost. They are called the Bible and they exist in many languages. Remember what I told you before? I am here to translate those books into the Canela language. Last week I translated the whole story about the death of Jesus."

The chief and the rest of the elders looked shocked. "So why were you just sitting there listening to us old men guessing at what might have happened? Quick! Run! Get those papers and read them to us. We want to know the facts."

A few minutes later, I was back. I handed out some carbon copies of the Passion and Easter story, even though at that time none of them could read. I showed them how to operate the cassette tape player on which I had recorded the translation. The rest of the evening and throughout the next day that cassette player went from the elders' group to the next younger age group, right through to the young initiates. They passed it from house to house until the batteries went dead.

This was the first time the Holy Spirit spoke Canela—the first time the whole village heard a major portion of God's Word in their own language. Although it would still be years before large numbers of Canelas would turn to follow God, this was a great start.

What bothers me is that today, 35 years later, millions of people in thousands of people groups are still just as confused and ignorant about Easter as those Canela elders were.

How much longer will they need to wait to hear that Jesus died and rose again for them?

And hear it in their own language?

⊹ Column 17 ⊹
Exercising Faith:
The Rest of the Story

My wife and I have been with Wycliffe, a faith mission, for more than 40 years. The traditional meaning of the term "faith mission" is "Workers do not get a salary, but are financially supported by gifts from churches, friends and family." It does mean this, but it also means a lot more.

Jo and I gave up a comfortable, prosperous future with home, family, friends and a lucrative career, believing God would move people to give enough money for us to live on and work with. That takes some faith. But it took a whole lot more faith to invest nearly 25 years to work with a minority language people group, to leave them with a Book, and to expect God to use it to change lives and transform that culture! This also needs to be included in the definition of "faith mission"—transformed lives and redeemed cultures through faith in God that comes by reading, understanding and obeying His Book.

There is even more to this concept of living by faith. Think of the 1 Kings 17 story of the prophet Elijah. After he told wicked King Ahab that God's judgment was coming on the land in the form of drought and famine, God sent him to live by a brook in a deserted ravine. There Elijah exercised his faith in his miracle-working God Who sent ravens to bring him bread and meat twice a day. Elijah's experience corresponds closely to the situation of Wycliffe missionaries who exercise their faith in their miracle-working God to move His people to send gifts.

Now read the rest of the story. The brook dried up, and God had a different plan. Elijah was sent to live with a widow and her son who were so poor they had flour and oil for only one more meal before they died of starvation. You know the story: "Make me a small loaf of bread first and bring it to me, then make some for your son and yourself." Exercise your faith in God Who says, "Neither your flour nor your oil will be used up until the time of famine is over" (1 Kings 17:13, 14, author's paraphrase). Elijah was not being rude, selfish or impolite; instead, he was giving the widow an opportunity to exercise her faith in God. She did and she lived.

The widow's experience corresponds closely to what financial partners do when they exercise their faith in their miracle-working God by giving money to His workers, the missionaries. With our focus so often on the missionary worker to exercise faith, we have lost sight of an important fact. Financial partners exercise faith too! It takes a lot of faith in a miracle-working God for His people to commit to financially support missions work in faraway, out of sight places like Africa and Asia.

Many churches are filled with people exercising their faith in a miracle-working God. Pastors preach the Word, exercising their faith that God will use it to change lives and redeem households. Testimonies abound of people exercising their faith to be physically healed.

But where are the testimonies of financial partners? Financial partners who exercise their faith to give, to give liberally, generously, faithfully and consistently? How many testimonies have you heard of people exercising their faith by giving far beyond what they had planned to give, and then God supplying their needs miraculously? I know it goes against many cultures, including my own, to talk about money and about our giving. But wouldn't it be an enormous encouragement to others to hear even anonymous, third-person stories of how God supplied the needs of those who gave sacrificially?

May God raise up thousands of financial partners who give to missions like the starving widow who gave her last meal to Elijah. I pray for millions of financial partners learning to live in the excitement of being faith partners with God in His work of providing the Bread of Life for every people group on earth.

⋄ COLUMN 18 ⋄
CHECK IT OUT FOR YOURSELF

I used to consider myself a pretty good communicator. Then one day, back in the 1970s, my dad and mom took me aside and said, "Jack, we had no idea that you and Jo lived like *that* in the Canela village. We didn't realize you and our grandkids lived in a hut with a dirt floor and dried mud walls. We didn't know that you had no privacy, no conveniences and no non-Canela friends anywhere near."

I couldn't believe my ears. These, after all, were my mom and dad: the recipients of scores of my letters during the previous six years. I had shown them hundreds of slides illustrating every aspect of our lives, and had told them dozens of stories. Jo and I had sent them numerous photographs, given them armfuls of native artifacts during our previous furlough, and answered tons of questions.

All that communication, however, was nothing compared to what they saw for themselves when they came to Brazil to visit us. It started when Dad walked around the Canela village and shook hands with hundreds of Canela men saying, "Ipe Prejaka mehum." (I am Jack's father.) As he saw what we saw, heard what we heard, smelled what we smelled, and began to feel what we felt, he finally began to understand.

I always encourage pastors and other leaders to widen their narrow worlds by going out to the mission field to see for themselves, thus obeying Jesus' words, "Open your eyes and look on the harvest fields" (John 4:35, author's paraphrase). Making a trip to a spiritually needy location in Africa or Asia under the guidance of an experienced missionary, as my dad and mom did, is a good start to widening your world. But it is not a panacea, a cure-all for the ignorance the North American church has toward the mission field.

One of my colleagues, a veteran missionary who trains nationals in Papua New Guinea, made some insightful comments on the difference between brief missions trips and living and working in a cross-cultural environment.

One furlough, he heard a representative from a certain mission agency preaching on the value of giving money to nationals in his agency. He told his hearers that sending money was the only logical way to be involved in missions. Going ourselves was not important since "we could do more with less by giving money."

At the end of his talk, my colleague asked him, "Have you lived overseas?" The answer was no. He had visited, but had never lived among nationals for an extended period. No wonder he felt discipleship and nurturing were not that important. His solution appealed to his audience, but his message was not balanced. A brief trip to a mission field without proper orientation and "on the ground" guidance can make the wrong impression.

When pastors and church leaders continue to suffer from shrunken vision, they cannot lead their churches into obeying the Great Commission. This has serious consequences. An Australian colleague told me his denomination was shrinking in both missions outlook and numbers, focusing on simply surviving as a church denomination. That describes a church already dead. Consider John Stott's description of the five-fold biblical missions focus:

1. The God of the Old Testament is a missionary God, calling one family in order to bless all the families of the earth.

2. The Christ of the Gospels is a missionary Christ; he sent the church out to witness.

3. The Spirit of the Acts is a missionary Spirit; he drove the church out from Jerusalem to Rome.

4. The church of the epistles is a missionary church, a worldwide community with a worldwide vocation.

5. The end of the Revelation is a missionary end, a countless throng from every nation.

Stott goes on to say: "So I think we have to say the religion of the Bible is a missionary religion. The evidence is overwhelming and irrefutable. Mission cannot be regarded as a regrettable lapse from tolerance (for cultures) or decency. Mission cannot be regarded as the hobby of a few fanatical eccentrics in the church. Mission lies at the heart of God and therefore at the very heart of the church. A church without mission is no longer a church. It is contradicting an essential part of its identity. The church *is* mission."[1]

Every pastor and leader of a Christian ministry organization needs to experience some cross-cultural missions for himself or herself. Just hearing and reading about it, even from people like me, who think they are great communicators, is not sufficient.

As Jesus said, "Open your eyes and look…"

1. John R. W. Stott, 'The Whole Christian', in *Proceedings of the International Conference of Christian Medical Students*, ed. Lee Moy Ng (London: ICCMS and Christian Medical Fellowship, 1980), 46. Reprinted in *Authentic Christianity* (Downers Grove, IL: InterVarsity Press, 1996), 315-316.

→ COLUMN 19 ←
MAMA AND THE WAR

Dear Mama,

Happy Mother's Day, Mama. And Happy Liberation Day! More than 60 years ago, Canadian soldiers fought their way through Holland to Hilversum, our town, and freed us from fear and oppression. I was seven years old when Papa took me to see the Canadian tanks growl along Main Street.

Thank you for shielding me from so much of the horror of war. I was only two years old when the enemy overran our country. You sheltered me, but you could not insulate yourself from the daily stress.

You and Papa tried to live a normal life. The year the war started, you gave me a little brother, and cared for him day and night for nine months until he finally died of an inoperable heart defect. I wonder if you ever got over that strain and loss. Two years later, you gave me a little sister, and two years after that another little brother. All this time you wondered where you would get enough food to feed us all.

I remember waking up many nights to the sound of gunshots in the neighbourhood. Eventually it became normal and I slept right through it. But did you? How could you, when you knew Papa was out there, in the night, after curfew, bartering for food? How could you sleep when you didn't know where he was, or if he was safe? How did you live through that time he was gone for weeks and finally arrived with one jug of cooking oil?

When the grain for porridge was gone and there were only two potatoes left in the bin, I didn't know. But you knew. In the meantime, Pake and Beppe, your parents in Friesland, had hidden a sack of potatoes in a fishing boat that was coming our way. You must have prayed so much for God's protection over that sack of potatoes. Thank you, Mama!

I ran to the house one afternoon, excitedly pounding on the door to be let in, shouting, "De moffen komen eraan!" (The Germans are coming!) You quickly yanked me indoors and shushed me, reminding me to whisper, not shout this warning. I explained that soldiers had blocked off both ends of the street and that they were picking up men to transport them to slave labour camps in Germany. Then I watched as Papa quickly dragged the buffet in the back room away from the wall, rolled back the carpet, yanked open a trapdoor, and clambered down into the darkness. I helped you push everything back into place.

I was only four years old and it didn't bother me that Papa lived under the floor so often. But no doubt it bothered you. How could you sleep when you knew that any night, at any moment, rifle butts could pound our front door and Papa would have to rush down the stairs into his hiding place?

In the last winter of the war, trains no longer ran into Germany: all the railway bridges had been bombed, and so the threat of slave labour raids stopped. Papa came out of hiding; we got our bicycles out of hiding too. One day Papa took me for a bike ride out into the country. When we returned, I excitedly told you about the fun day we had.

"The airplanes came and Papa and I threw down our bikes, and we jumped down into one of those holes beside the road. And I saw them shoot at the airplanes. And they hit one and I saw the smoke, and I saw the parachutes. And then we got to the farmer, and he put the rabbit in the bottom of Papa's bike carrier and covered it up with vegetables. And then the soldier stopped us and poked his gun among the vegetables. And then the rabbit poked his nose out and sniffed the gun. And then Papa gave the soldier a package of cigarettes. And then the soldier walked away."

No doubt you prayed hard during that "fun" day: not only for our safety, but that the rabbit would not be confiscated. Thank you, Mama.

Then, finally, liberation! No more hiding under the floor. No more hunger. No more waking up from shots in the night. No more confiscation raids, for food, bicycles, radios and men. No more listening to the BBC news in Dutch on earphones from a secret radio hidden above the linen closet. No more curfews. No more food smuggling. No more trains of boxcars with begging hands sticking out through the cracks in the boards. No more women and children only in public.

Thank you, Mama, for looking after me during those terrible years.

Your son,
Jack

PS: And you 7,600 Canadian mamas—you whose soldier sons died to liberate our country—Mama and I continue to thank you for your sacrifice.

DRIVE AROUND THOSE POTHOLES

I love books, but not bookkeeping. During the decades we worked in Brazil, one of the jobs I most hated was processing my monthly ministry receipts. The Brazilian tax authorities required us to copy everything in triplicate, with the exact code numbers, in order to turn them in as income tax deductions. No errors, cross-outs, or erasures permitted. Aaargh!

This loathsome task forced me to operate right in the middle of some of my worst weaknesses: arithmetic, exact details, accuracy with numbers, and mind-numbing repetition. A morning spent in this drudgery ruined me for the entire day. Moreover, I did not suffer in silence. My wife will bear witness.

Imagine, therefore, my joy and delight when Jan, our centre bookkeeper, noticing my obvious distress, made me an offer I could not refuse.

"We are due to go on furlough next year and need some new, up-to-date stories for our talks," she said. "I will process your monthly receipts for you if you write me a story from your experiences in the Canela Bible translation program."

Yippee! Clutching my folder of receipts, I bustled home, sat down at the typewriter and wrote not one, but two stories. Back I ran to the bookkeeper's office, and handed in the receipts and the stories. She was happy. I was delighted, and walked away as if on air, freed of that odious task. By the start of her furlough she had a collection of 30 stories, and I had the start of a large resource file for speeches, articles and books.

It is axiomatic for good managers to work within their strengths and to staff for their weaknesses. That is why it jars me to hear people say, "I dislike this task and have such a hard time doing it, I am going to have to take a course to learn how to do it well."

Training to improve your weaknesses is like stopping to fill potholes in a long road: an endless, hopeless, energy-draining task. Better to learn where the potholes are and drive around them. Train in the area of your strengths and talents and you become even better at them. This means we all need to know where we shine and where we stink.

At the last Wycliffe Canada annual general meeting, we honoured five people for 40 years of service, and another couple for 50 years of work, and none of them are retiring yet. What is their secret of a long productive life? We found out when they told us about their assignments.

For most of their time in Wycliffe, these people had worked well within their areas of strengths. They all had different jobs, and each had made several career changes, sometimes discovering unknown talents and giftings. They also displayed godly attitudes such as love for others, and a thorough understanding that only the Holy Spirit can produce spiritual results.

God has given each of us a few natural talents, one or two spiritual gifts and some personality strengths with which to serve Him. Just a few. For every one thing we do well, there will be 50 we don't do well. They are potholes in our road. Stay away from them as much as possible. Management gurus tell us we should be happy if we have a job where we can spend 70 percent of our time doing things we like to do and are good at.

So what about the other 30 percent? Well, sometimes God just needs a human being with the right attitude, at the right time and in the right place. I have no giftings in evangelism, but within months of my coming to know Christ at the age of 14, God used me to lead my sister to Him. I have no natural talents in counselling, yet in one of my leadership positions God used me to deal effectively with a most serious and difficult situation. The 15 minutes I spend shaking hands and chatting at the door with 200 strangers drains more of my energy than speaking to them for an hour. But God helps me to do both.

God is God, and He can do whatever He wants with us. But when He equips us with certain strengths, talents and spiritual gifts, He expects us to use them. The oft-repeated semi-joking statement, "I love doing A and am good at it, but, of course, when I went to the mission field I had to do B," borders on blasphemy.

Yes, there will be times we have to do something we are not fitted for, but God will not fill our lives with those things. Speaking of which, I need to stop what I love doing—writing this column. It's the first week of the month again, and I have to process my receipts for the ministry expense report to satisfy Canadian tax authorities. Sigh.

PRAYER AND PING-PONG BALLS

You know the quote, "I have so much to do today; I will need to spend the first three hours in prayer." The first time I read that oxymoronic statement attributed to the great reformer, Martin Luther, it blew me away. I much preferred his other quote on prayer: "The fewer the words, the better the prayer."

By the way, this is about personal organization, so if you are never overwhelmed by the things in your life, save time and skip to the next piece.

One day I caught myself working hard, but still feeling guilty. What was going on? While preparing for Sunday's speaking engagement, I felt pressure to finish the carpentry work in the hall. While hauling water to fill our cistern, I scolded myself for not studying to improve my writing skills. While dealing with a list of emails, I kept thinking I should be helping my wife move some bushes. And so on.

Then I remembered a game we used to play as kids. One person would take a five-gallon can or even a garbage can, put some Ping-Pong balls in it, close the lid and turn around to face his friends. He would shake the can and everybody standing around would hear the Ping-Pong balls bouncing and rattling inside. Their job was to guess how many balls were in the can. They usually guessed way too many. It's unbelievable how a strong shaker can make three or four Ping-Pong balls sound like 20 or 30. I used to make a lot of money that way. (Juuust kidding!)

Satan is an expert can-shaker. He overwhelms us by making us believe our lives are filled with dozens of problems to solve, duties to perform and responsibilities to fulfill. We wake up, stagger off to the bathroom, and before we have finished washing our faces, we're already thinking of the many things we need to do that day. That's when we are least likely to follow Martin Luther's famous example of three hours of prayer.

Having entered codgerhood some years ago, I don't need as much sleep as I did when I was younger. It's much easier to get out of bed, sit down in a comfortable chair, read my Bible and pray through the day. Sometimes I turn on my laptop and start a file called, "Counting the Ping-Pong Balls." I list every possible thing filling my mind.

I then sort them out a bit, and am always amazed at how few there are. Satan was up to his old tricks again, making me believe I had dozens of situations to deal with when there were only five or six. Usually I need to handle only one or two that day.

Then I schedule a time to do them. (You already know that To Do lists don't work, not unless you schedule each item to be done at a certain time on a certain day.) While I think of these items, writing the lists and scheduling them into my day, I pray.

No, not with my eyes closed. Not kneeling. Not with my hands folded. Not even reading a well-thought-through written prayer, even though these are all great ways to pray. No, I look like an ordinary businessman filling in his appointment calendar. But I do think through each item carefully. I reflect on each person I will meet with or write to. I take each situation on my list and connect God to each item. Believe it or not, that is prayer.

Richard J. Foster, one of my favourite authors, agrees with me: "Countless people pray far more than they know. Often they have such a stained-glass image of prayer that they fail to recognize what they are experiencing as prayer, and so condemn themselves for not praying."[1]

I can now visualize Luther in his study: He reads the Scriptures, praises God for Who He is. He thanks God for another day and jots down notes for another great hymn. Feeling overwhelmed with things to do, he defeats Satan by counting the sixteenth century equivalent of Ping-Pong balls. He lists his duties and responsibilities. He ponders the situations he needs to deal with and writes out the scriptural principles to keep in mind. He reflects on the people he needs to meet that day and commits each meeting to God. After three hours of this, he is fully prepared, well prayed up and ready to take on the day.

That's an example anyone can follow.

1. Richard J. Foster, *Prayer: Finding the Heart's True Home* (San Francisco: HarperSanFranscisco, 1992), preface.

A MUSICAL LESSON IN PARTNERSHIP

My Canela Indian mother, the one who adopted me, ran into our mud-walled house shouting, "Quick, you and your family, come with me up to the central plaza! It's about to start!" Seeing my puzzled look, she added, "No time to explain."

A few minutes later we joined our Canela family members, a group of about 100, at the edge of the circular plaza in the centre of our village in Brazil. We stood in that part of the circle nearest to our families' homes. The other seven groups of villagers did the same, each group spaced around the circle, each closest to their respective family houses.

Then our family started singing a song. I noticed that the other groups were singing too, each one its own song. For a few minutes, I stepped away from my group and listened to all seven choirs grimly competing with the others. It was awful. Out-of-sync rhythms! Clashing tunes! Dissonance! Disharmony! Discord! I was glad to step back into my own group, out of the cacophony, and bellow out our own familiar song.

Suddenly the village song leader walked into the plaza. Shaking his rattle, he stepped up to one of the groups and began singing a different song. The group stopped singing its own song and sang the leader's song. Thus he went from group to group, teaching each one his song. Finally, all the groups sang the new song together. What a difference! Beautiful harmony, solid rhythm and singers with smiling, happy faces.

"Okay, it's done. Let's go," said my Canela mother, tugging at my arm. Each group marched back to its own group of palm-thatched houses, still singing in unity. Then came the explanations.

She told me that the Canela people are remnants of seven related, but distinct, groups. They survived attacks from enemies and suffered epidemics, coming together many seasons ago. They brought their own customs, dialects and songs that they still remember, even though they have been living together for generations.

"This song ceremony reminds us that we started different from each other but have learned to work together," my mother continued. "Together we can do things that no single group could possibly do alone. That is why this village is now large and growing. We feel safe in our strength, and with large gardens we don't suffer hunger anymore."

Safety and survival are the main goals of the Canela people. The Christian Church has even greater goals—evangelize the world and disciple the nations. These tasks demand that someone provides the Word of God in the heart language of every person on earth.

We need to learn from the Canelas. The groups stopped singing their own song and learned a new one. What they *were* didn't change; they continued to be Canelas. But they changed what they *did*. Instead of each group sticking to itself and promoting its own interest, it cooperated with the others and focused on the main goal.

Praise God, this is starting to happen in the world of cross-cultural missions and Bible translation.

- Wycliffe partners with scores of other mission agencies and organizations.

- Denominations of every sort collaborate, realizing they cannot complete the job of world evangelization by working alone.

- Groups cooperate instead of compete.

- They use the strengths in one organization to make up for the weaknesses in another organization.

- Nationals are part of the leadership of missions work on the fields.

- Young people are getting their first taste of missions work together with retired folk.

- Both groups serve on the field together with local people and with career missionaries from around the world.

- Like the Canela groups, these groups do not change who they *are*, but what they *do*.

Jesus, who prayed for unity of purpose and action, is no doubt pleased. We who are working together are excited with our mission on earth—to sing one song together—today working together on earth, and eventually worshiping together in heaven.

PEDAL DEXTERITY AND WD-40

"So what country did your parents work in as missionaries?" the student asked.

Our daughter Valorie looked surprised. "What makes you think my folks were missionaries?"

"Well," he said, "as we were standing here talking, your pencil fell to the floor from the stack of books in your arms. I was about to pick it up for you, when you kicked off your sandal, picked up the pencil with your toes, reached down with one hand, took your pencil and slipped your foot back into your sandal. During the whole process, you never missed a word in our conversation or lost eye contact with me. I figured you must be a missionary kid. They run around barefoot all their lives: their feet are like another pair of hands."

No young couple will commit their lives to cross-cultural missions work so that their kids can develop great pedal dexterity. But neither should they hesitate to accept an overseas assignment in missions for the sake of their children. God blesses MKs and makes them special in many positive ways.

Our daughters lived with us in the Canela village in Brazil at least three months each year. Even during their elementary school years, they learned up close about the pain and joy of birth, the frustration of sickness and the finality of death. They cried as playmates died, then helped to bury them, kneeling down and scooping handfuls of earth onto the grave mound along with the rest of the mourners.

One furlough, my family and I visited yet another large church. In the crowded vestibule after the morning service, I stood by our display table and answered questions. Suddenly I overheard our 13-year-old daughter talking about "our translation work." There she was, explaining the biblical basis of Bible translation to three adult men. I looked around for the others. Twelve-year old Leanne talked animatedly with an older couple who listened intently. Off to one side our 10-year-old Cheryl explained things on our display to the parents of a small family. We heard it often during furloughs: "Your daughters talk with adults!" and "Until I talked with your daughter, I had not had an intelligent conversation with a teenager for months."

Years later, Leanne, our middle daughter, discussing basic human needs, could not believe what she was hearing from her college friends in southern California. Finally she burst out, "You don't *need* a swimming pool! People need drinking water. People need air. People need sun, sleep and food. Nobody *needs* a swimming pool!"

MKs tend to know who they are. They understand themselves and are competent and confident. This week my oldest daughter, a pastor's wife, checked her purse. She pulled out a household-sized, blue-and-yellow spray can of WD-40, the world's best-known spray lubricant, and put it back on the shelf. Seeing the look of surprise on my face she explained, "The door on the prayer meeting room has been squeaking worse lately. It disturbs the rest of us when latecomers arrive. So last night I took along my WD-40 and fixed it."

Missionary kids become part of vital ministry. They develop a personal relationship with God, and learn to pray for clothing, food and basic health. They know the difference between *wants* and *needs*. They learn the value of money. They can talk with anyone. They know how to live life…anywhere.

"I will be with you always," Jesus promised those who leave home to evangelize the world. This promise includes their kids. No one needs to be afraid of the dangers on the field, or the isolation from home culture, and how these will affect their children. Where Jesus is, is a good place to bring up kids. Even on the mission field.

Oh, and don't forget the benefit of having an extra pair of hands at the end of their legs.

A TALE OF TWO PASTORS

"It was the best of times, it was the worst of times…" Thus Charles Dickens began his famous 119-word first sentence in his equally famous historical novel *A Tale of Two Cities*. He continues with "…it was the age of wisdom, it was the age of foolishness…" and so on for five more sets of contrasts.

I think of that passage when I remember what happened during one of the "missions saturation" weekends that Jo and I put on in churches during our furloughs. On Friday, Jo spoke at a women's tea; that night I challenged young people by telling missions stories. Saturday morning I cast vision for Bible translation at a men's breakfast and that night did a monolingual language-learning demonstration at an all-church public rally. On Sunday morning, Jo spoke at the younger kids' Sunday school open session, while I spoke at the older kids' session. Jo taught one adult class, I taught another; I preached at both Sunday morning services, and in the evening I spoke at a potluck fellowship.

Then, on Monday, the pastor returned from an out-of-town convention where he had been all weekend. Several elders phoned with a positive report on what had happened while he was away. Sunday school teachers and missions committee members were bubbling with inspiration and encouragement. Thirteen young people had indicated they wanted to give their lives for cross-cultural missions. *It was the best of times…*

The pastor, however, having missed it all, was not impressed. What's more, he did not feel it was his responsibility, or his church's, to follow up the young people who had experienced an encounter with the Lord of the Harvest. As a result, most of the effect of that weekend dissipated. *It was the worst of times…*

That situation made such an impact on me that for a while I refused to accept invitations to speak at a church if the pastor would not be there.

Fortunately, there are other "best of times" pastors, who do understand that the Church, not mission agencies, is responsible to God for the global missions task. I remember doing a similar weekend in another church where Jim, a high school student, was about to leave on an all summer missions trip to Africa. Before the pastor introduced me to speak in the Sunday morning service, he and Jim stood on the platform and the pastor said, "Folks, you know Jim, and you know what kind of a computer whiz he is. He could easily get a job this summer and make some good money for a new computer or a better car. But he believes God wants him to go overseas and substitute for a missionary computer technician who is coming home on a short furlough. The elders and I have affirmed that vision. He has been praying for the money needed for this trip, and some of you have helped to finance him. He is still short, however, and his flight is this Wednesday, so during the offering after the message, please be generous."

I preached, referring to Jim and his ministry during the message. The pastor appealed to the people once again before taking up the offering. That Sunday night the pastor stood on the platform again. He repeated the same story, only this time, with his arm around Jim's shoulders, the pastor concluded, "…and if there still is not enough money for Jim's trip after tonight's offering, Jim and I will come to visit some of you at your place of business or in your homes on Monday to ask for specific amounts."

That Wednesday Jim was on the plane!

It was the best of times…

CHILDREN NEED A MAN IN THEIR LIVES

- Twenty-five million children in North America have *no* reason to celebrate Father's Day.

- One out of three children grows up in a home with no father present, because of abandonment, separation or divorce. Twelve million children have not seen their fathers in the past year. A quarter of these absent fathers live in a different state or province than their kids.[1]

- Nine out of ten runaways come from such homes. So do seven out of ten high school dropouts and eight out of ten youths currently in prison.[2]

Our disintegrating North American society may need to adopt something from Canela culture. Every Canela home has at least one male figure, often two or three, with significant responsibilities in bringing up children who are not their own biological offspring.

Canela society is mother-oriented; the daughters live with or near their mothers. When a girl marries, her bridegroom comes to live with her in her mother's home, but he maintains strong connections with his boyhood home.

That is why, in traditional Canela society, the man who has the most influence during the growing-up years of a boy is not necessarily the biological father, but rather one or more of his mother's brothers. To a lesser extent, this is true for girls too. The child's biological father performs the same function for his sisters' children back in his boyhood home.

A Canela child, therefore, develops a strong relationship, not with his biological father, but with his uncle, his mother's brother. It is the uncle, not the father, who disciplines the child, teaches him socially approved behaviour and skills in hunting, fishing, food gathering. The uncle demonstrates the value of work as he works with the boy to clear land, build a house and plant a garden.

In contrast, the Jewish culture was father-oriented. Young couples often started married life in the home of the groom's father. Some current Western societies are father-oriented. Others focus more on the new family without strong ties to either originating family.

When we planned to translate the Lord's Prayer, we thoroughly studied this mother-oriented aspect of Canela culture.

"Our Father who is in heaven": does that connect with Canela culture? Surely it would make more impact to translate, "Our Uncle who is in heaven"? But if God is our heavenly Uncle, our mother's brother, then who is our heavenly Mother? And who would be her Husband, and thus our Father? Whoa!

Although we abandoned the "heavenly Uncle" idea and focused on the Fatherhood of God when we translated the Scriptures, the Canela concept of several men responsible to raise a child is valuable.

Every child needs a father figure who shares responsibility with the child's mother to bring him or her up. If the biological father is absent, then, as among the Canela, some other man needs to commit to this responsibility.

It happens sometimes in our society with good results. One third-grade child wrote, "The dad in my life isn't really my dad. He's my grandpa, but he's been like a dad to me since before I was born. I wouldn't trade him for all the dads in the world."[1]

According to Psalm 68:4–5 God relates well to orphans, those bereft of their fathers: "Enjoy God, cheer when you see Him! Father of orphans, champion of widows is God in His holy house" (The Message).

God loves to use His people in His work. Here is one way to extend the Fatherhood of God: We who are children of Abraham by faith inherit God's promise to Abraham, "In you all the families of the earth will be blessed" (Gen. 12:3, NASB).

Is there a better way for a Christian man to bless a family whose father is absent than to commit to help the mother train and influence the children?

1. Patrick F. Fagan and Kirk A. Johnson, "Marriage: The Safest Place fo Women and Children," *Heritage Foundation Backgrounder* 1535 (2002).

2. Kathryn Mulolani, "Where Are the Fathers?", *Testimony* (June 2005).

GOD IS SERIOUS ABOUT GLOBAL MISSIONS: HIS CHURCH IS NOT

After 2,000 years of "doing missions as usual" it is time to get serious.

One billion adults have never had a chance to learn to read. Billions of people are locked into Islam, Hinduism and other major world religions. The physical and spiritual needs in places such as Africa and Asia are still immense. Two hundred and seventy million people, separated into more than 2,500 language groups, most of them unwritten, still do not have one verse of God's Word in the language that speaks to them most powerfully.[1] The Great Commission to evangelize the world and disciple the nations is not yet complete.

Meanwhile, every Sunday in well-evangelized, affluent Western nations, millions of born-again Christians worship in thousands of churches of dozens of denominations. On weekdays, they live good lives and are a witness to God in their neighbourhood. All this is good.

Something, however, needs to happen to jog the Church out of its "missions as usual" mode. The Church around the world will not complete the Great Commission until it takes cross-cultural missions as seriously as God does.

I have some practical ideas. What do you think would happen in the Church and the world of missions if:

1. Bible schools and seminaries refuse to accept a student until he or she has served in a cross-cultural mission field for a minimum of three months?

2. Churches grant voting rights only to members who are active in an approved ministry and give a significant proportion of their income to God's work?

3. Seminaries make a year of cross-cultural missionary service a

mandatory part of the curriculum and part of every degree?

4. Churches call as pastors only those people who have served at least two years on the foreign mission field?

5. Every pastor plans one full year of missionary service in a less developed country every ten years?

6. Mission agencies see themselves as servants of the Church, not as independents and competitors?

7. Churches consistently teach biblical stewardship of time and money and the church leaders are clearly seen to practice both?

8. Churches stop spending most of God's money on themselves instead of on the poor and needy around the world?

9. Churches discipline members who live in immorality, who are steeped in materialism or deep in consumer debt, or who live selfish lives?

10. The church guarantees the basic living and travel expenses of every secondary school graduate who is a member of the church, if he or she wants to serve for one year overseas as a missionary with a reputable mission organization, and if he or she meets the church and mission agency standards?

11. Church denominations commit themselves to staff and fund a fair proportion of the critical, strategic and foundational work of Bible translation still left undone in the world?

12. Every church has a team of volunteers trained to promote local outreach and cross-cultural missions in every area of church life?

13. Mission organizations and church denominations work together to challenge, evaluate and train young people to serve in cross-cultural missions and to guide older folk to finance missions?

14. Christian families plan as enthusiastically for their next kingdom-building venture as they do for their next home improvement project?

15. Elders practice biblical oversight and prayerfully encourage

those young people in the congregation that they sense need to make foreign missions a career?

What would happen in the Church? There would be revival. There would be an explosion of church growth.

The needs of the world would soon be met, the Great Commission would be completed and the Lord of the Harvest would say, "At last! The work is done!"

1. Wycliffe Bible Translators, Intl. annual statistics 2005 (Dallas, TX).

WHAT FEAR DRIVES US TO OUR KNEES IN PRAYER?

I respected my Bible college roommate. Eugene knew his Bible backward and forward. Each morning I woke to see him on his knees praying through the Bible passage he had just read. I greatly admired him.

One day he criticized me strongly. "Jack, you are so proud. You're so full of yourself." We often punched each other verbally, but this time I saw no smile.

"Why do you say that?" I asked, not feeling particularly proud, but fully aware of my robust Dutch ego.

"You're going to preach at the rescue mission tonight and you've hardly even prayed. You are so confident and proud, how do you expect God to use you?"

He had me there. It had been his turn to preach the week before. Day after day, I had seen him on his knees, agonizing in prayer for hours, while he prepared his talk. In comparison, my prayer before putting together my speeches was usually short and businesslike: "Okay, Lord. Here we go. It is my turn to preach to these men. I don't know anything about them, but You do. They are grown men, living a hard life, while I am just a teenage kid. I have nothing to give them except the truth of Your Word. So please put some ideas into my head right now, and some illustrations, and I'll stand up there and talk. If something in my life displeases You, show me now so I can confess it and make it right. I want these men to hear Your Spirit in their hearts while they hear my voice in their ears. Make something happen in their lives tonight. Amen."

Then I would sit down, look up some Bible verses, write an outline, jot down an illustration or two and head downtown. Sure, my heart pounded as I sat on the front row during the hymn sing. My hands felt cold, and I felt incredibly alert. That was just normal preaching excitement. After all, my hearers might think God's thoughts for the first time in their lives. Who knows what effect this would have on them? Sometimes people would respond to the invitation to follow God, sometimes they did not. I left that for Him to work out.

With my roommate's question still ringing in my ears, I looked him in the eye and said, "We both know you pray way more than I do when you prepare a speech. But last weekend you took the motor out of your pickup truck and replaced it with another one—how much did you pray about that?"

He looked a bit surprised and said, "I didn't pray at all. I just did it."

"Speaking in public is as natural to me as doing major mechanical work is to you. If I had to take out a motor, I would be praying before, during and afterward. I would be terrified I would not get it back together right and would be forced to call a mechanic to fix it. He would laugh at me and I would be embarrassed. Maybe that is the same reason you pray to God to help you make it through your speech."

During the past 50 years, things have changed for both of us. Eugene has made hundreds of public speeches. He probably feels much more confident now. Although I have never taken the motor out of a truck, I have spent hundreds of hours doing mechanical things with wrenches. Sometimes things even work after I am through with them.

I am no longer an inexperienced teenage kid. I now have hundreds of stories that testify to what God has done in my life and in the lives of those touched by my wife's and my ministry. Testimonial stories have supernatural power. As St. John reports, "They overcame him [Satan] by the blood of the Lamb and by the word of their testimony" (Rev. 12:11).

My prayer while preparing my speeches has not changed much. God still knows my audience much better than I ever will. I still depend on the truth of His Word and on His Holy Spirit to speak to people's hearts. And I continue to invite God to show me things in my life that displease Him so I can make them right.

If Eugene could see me now, he might be tempted to still make the same criticism. I have even greater confidence in my talents as a public speaker. Yet I know that unless God's Holy Spirit speaks into the lives of my hearers, my stories are merely Christian entertainment.

The fear of that drives me to my knees.

⊹ Column 28 ⊹
God Boring? Never!

The moment I stepped off the plane in Trinidad it hit me again. I was overwhelmed with the diversity of people in the Piarco airport, on the streets of Port of Spain and in the stores. Skin color of every variety. Bodies of every possible size, never mind all the different body shapes. And then there are the faces, from old and wrinkled great-grandmothers to the peachy smooth cheeks of the babies they hold. What an enormous variety—but wait, there's more!

All these human beings, so diverse in many ways, are built on the same pattern: one head, two eyes, one nose, two nostrils, a pair of hands and a pair of legs…Amazing, such variety within a basic pattern. Do I need to talk about fingers and the system of individualized whorls and loops that makes every one of the six billion people on the planet unique? Then there is every human being's individualized DNA sequence. (You can tell I keep up with the crime and police news—well, at least with the TV crime detective shows!)

What a wonderful God we have! To design a creation based on such a simple pattern, but with infinite variety and diversity within the pattern. Just like the multi-zillions of snowflakes in Canada. No one has ever found one exactly alike, yet they are all built on the same six-sided crystal pattern.

Of course, it goes way beyond bodies and snow. Every aspect of every individual, patterned after God Himself, with a body, a soul and a spirit, has his or her own personality, qualities, giftings and strengths all coming together to make a unique individual. We do not serve a boring God. He loves diversity.

Obviously since no individuals are alike in every respect, no groups are alike either. Families of individuals differ. No two churches are exactly alike, even within the same denomination, in the same town, and of the same size. Organizations, agencies, companies, missions—each has its own intrinsic qualities.

Oh, and did I mention the heterogeneity of indigenous people groups, all over the world? Speaking their own unique language, each with their own special culture, their own fears and hang-ups, their own history of triumphs and failures, their own specific environments... No wonder they need their own translation of the Word.

Sometimes, when I am tired, I wish there wasn't quite so much diversity. If only I could deal with staff or congregations as if they were all identical. Just think, when one was convinced, all would be convinced. But that would just make leadership and communication boring.

No, the miscellany of responses, even to these simple articles that I write, makes our lives worth living. And it draws me closer to the Creator of all this variegated diversity. He who created every person an individual and puts diversity in everything else invites us to work together with Him, to bring people of every language to Himself.

Nothing boring about that!

❖ Column 29 ❖
Giving to Charity or Building the Kingdom?

Imagine that you are handy with tools. You fix that dripping tap in the bathroom. You repair the broken chair in the kitchen. You even sew some of your own clothes. Then one day you wake up with a toothache. You need a tooth filled—something you can't fix yourself. So you make the trip to the dentist, and after he does what you cannot do for yourself, the receptionist hands you the bill. Then imagine you say to the receptionist:

"I have the money to pay this bill in my pocket, but I notice Dr. Pullem drives a much nicer car than I do. His house is much larger than mine, and I am sure he makes much more money than I do. Therefore, I am not paying his bill." What do you think would happen? In many places, that kind of attitude could land you in jail.

So obviously no one acts like this. Right? Wrong! I see this attitude displayed by people in every country I visit, particularly in the less affluent regions. I hear it coming out of the mouths of pastors. I hear it from church people, from missions volunteers, and even from our own Wycliffe members.

One pastor looked at the financial support figure required by Wycliffe for a highly trained, well-qualified young family going to serve on the other side of the world to train nationals and said, "What? That's more money than I get."

He was right. The missionary family had a high support figure. But the pastor didn't think of the many relevant factors: both adults would work full time in the ministry; the children would need to attend expensive international schools to meet their home country's academic standards; the family would have major travel expenses; the cost of living on the field would be much higher than at home; there would be numerous ministry expenses, etc.

A church member read in a newsletter that the missionary he supports plans to complete a Ph.D. study program. Although the missionary explained that the government of the country where he is teaching and doing translation work requires him to have these academic credentials in order to keep his visa, the supporter says, "Why should I pay for someone else to get a Ph.D.? I am still paying off the loan I took out to pay for my own medical degree."

He was right. But he needed to remember that he is working as a medical doctor and is making good money. But a Ph.D. in linguistics does not help the missionary earn a higher salary. Missionaries get not what they are worth, but what they need.

These situations illustrate a basic misconception about giving to missions. Charity is the Christian ministry of helping poor people meet basic human needs—the "haves" helping the "have nots." Giving to charity is the duty and privilege of every Christian. As Mother Teresa put it, we can see the face of Jesus in the face of those who suffer poverty. God's reward for giving to the poor is that the giver lays up treasure in heaven.

Money given to a Wycliffe missionary, however, is not charity in the sense of giving money to those poorer than you. When you give money to advance cross-cultural foreign missions, you give to God in a special way. You fund the kingdom-building mandate Jesus gave His Church in the Great Commission. Through your gifts you join Him in His kingdom-building work.

Wycliffe missionaries and other missionary professionals are well trained and perform work in cross-cultural missions on your behalf. They remind me of those skilled Israelite craftsmen and artisans who built the tabernacle in the wilderness. Those ancient workers were supplied with everything they needed by the people on whose behalf they worked.

Cross-cultural missionaries, like your dentist, do a job you cannot do yourself.

And, like your dentist, they need to be compensated.

THE WORMS ARE WAITING

What is it with this North American mania for watching reality TV?

Pastors and parents, teachers and leaders need to capitalize on this opportunity to present the challenge of doing perilous exploits for Jesus.

Every week multimillions of North Americans, including millions of churchgoers, watch young people compete in bizarre situations. My reaction as a veteran missionary is "Ho hum."

All these freakish situations are ordinary, everyday stuff for thousands of missionaries. Cross-cultural missionaries routinely live, work and bring up their families under conditions even more weird than any of the ones depicted in the television shows.

That show *Survivor*, for instance: so people are lost in a jungle. Yes, and what pioneer missionary has not been lost in some desolate area? I vividly remember being lost for most of one day while walking alone the 70 kilometres to the Canela village. A friend of ours, trying to cross the mouth of the Amazon in a small riverboat filled with his family, got caught in a storm and ended up in the Atlantic Ocean. Another family, hundreds of kilometres from the nearest town, coped without their supplies after their pole and thatch house burned down. Now that is survival!

Then there is *The Amazing Race*—traveling in every type of conveyance through foreign countries. What's the big deal? Missionaries do this all the time, while pregnant, and with preschool kids who are suffering from constant diarrhoea. They suffer the blinding headaches of falciparum malaria while keeping track of baggage. Baggage that is routinely lost for weeks. I am not making this up.

One of our Wycliffe missionary families traveled up a river in a dugout canoe for two weeks each time they went to the village. They used to tie a rope to their adventurous water-loving toddler so they could haul him back into the canoe before the piranhas got him.

Oh yes, and that show *Fear Factor* where participants eat bugs, or worms, or walk on narrow beams at a great height and have to deal with snakes and rats. I know of no missionary who has not had frequent encounters with these things. Noisy rats used to wake us up at night. So, while still lying in bed, I shot rats right off the pole rafters of our palm-leaf roof. Our preschool girls sleeping in their hammocks in the same room would wake up at the bang of the .22 calibre pistol, and then peacefully fall asleep again knowing it was just Daddy shooting rats again.

For personal encounters of the snake kind, nothing beats a couple of missionaries sitting around sipping coffee and swapping tales. Have I told you about my stingray attack? Want to see my scar? Oh, and about eating freaky food, ask any cross-cultural missionary; she will have you gagging in no time.

Thousands of today's cross-cultural missionaries come from Asia, South America and Africa. You should hear them talk about our bland Western food. No wonder Koreans growing up eating kimchi every day—that's spicy fermented cabbage—find much of our Western food as tasteless as raw egg whites.

There is a good reason that these reality TV shows fascinate viewers. They resonate with a desire deep within each human being. Every one of us wants to be significant in some way: to be uniquely valuable, or do something memorable. That is why there is no lack of candidates to participate in these bizarre TV shows. Viewers vicariously take part in all the stunts. Hence their popularity.

Where does this need for significance come from? God gave us this desire. People are already valuable because He loves us. Nothing we do can add to His love for us. Jesus, however, wants us to follow Him and join *The Amazing Race* to evangelize the world. He will help us to *Survive* attacks from Satan, and conquer all our *Fear Factors* in order to disciple the nations. He invites us to be involved as He builds His Church around the world.

Although reality television shows are a pale copy of the reality of cross-cultural missions, there is a close comparison.

The participants in the TV shows team up with a partner and organize themselves into teams. That is practical missions theology. Jesus said He would be our Partner in the hazardous task of worldwide evangelization. He would never leave us. We are part of a worldwide team, the Church.

The challenge to take on perilous tasks goes out on these television shows every week. But in the churches of our land, where is the challenge to risk danger to accomplish great things for God?

Pastors, leaders, teachers and parents need to throw out the missionary challenge to young people to take on the dangerous worldwide task of missions. And not just once a year during Missions Sunday. We need to regularly hear sermons on the thrill of going into places fraught with danger, and running huge risks for a great reward.

When pastors challenge people like that, many react positively. Not only in North America, but increasingly in former mission fields, people are responding to the challenge to get involved in cross-cultural missions. Some countries have the slogan, "From Mission Field, to Mission Force."

Enough of watching people do startling things for money. Let's get personally involved. The worms are waiting; so are the heavenly rewards.

IMPROVE THE SILENCE

Christian ministry organizations like Wycliffe check applicants for five essential personal characteristics. I call them the Vital Five C's: Christian Character, Competence, Calling, Compatibility and Communication. The first four are obvious. No ministry organization wants workers who are dishonest or unforgiving. Nor do they want people who cannot do the job, or those who are unwilling to make personal sacrifices, or who can't get along with other personalities, races or nationalities.

Given the other four C's are present, you may not think verbally interacting with others is all that important. Yet without free, easy and honest communication, relationships between people shrivel up and die. This is true for everything from marriages to churches and business organizations.

We can all think of instances when it is hard to speak. Having offended someone, I need to apologize. That is not easy. (It is not as difficult as asking for directions when I am lost, but that is another subject.)

Even when we want to make a positive contribution to a relationship, we sometimes hesitate to speak. Let's face it, if you open your mouth or write a letter, you run the risk of being misunderstood, possibly even criticized. If you say nothing, or write nothing, you're safe. Yet no business, or marriage, ever grew and prospered without the verbal input of the people involved. We all need each other's ideas and insights. We often discover and develop ideas through debate.

Talking in order to gossip is, of course, not what I am advocating. ("If you can't say anything nice, better say nothing at all," was the philosophy of Thumper's mother in the classic Disney film *Bambi*.) Nor is opening your mouth in anger: "Speak when you're angry and you'll make the best speech you'll ever regret." This echoes the advice from James 1:19: "Be quick to listen, slow to speak and slow to become angry." Numerous folk sayings underline the idea that in such cases keeping quiet is better than speaking: for instance, the Vermont proverb, "Don't talk unless you can improve the silence."

Relationships need spontaneous communication: sharing thoughts in a positive, up-building way; adding ideas; contributing to an ongoing discussion. That is how we all relate to each other and learn. That is how ideas are shaped and developed. But unless our attitude is right, our comment may not be well received. The biblical command is to "speak the truth in love." A Chinese proverb says, "Speak the truth, and run."

Sharing our thoughts is risky. I know. I do it regularly in public speeches. A thousand people read my weekly email columns. Each time I write a column or stand up to speak, I feel as if I am taking off some of my clothes, since I reveal something about myself in everything I say and write.

Plutarch, a Greek philosopher who lived about 50 years before Christ, put it this way: "In words are seen the state of mind and character and disposition of the speaker." That is scary stuff for every speaker and writer. But it is worth it. Not just for the satisfaction of seeing an audience listening intently, or reading the positive comments from readers, but knowing that in communicating my thoughts I have at least tried to improve the silence.

There may be scores of other valid reasons for not sharing your opinion in a discussion, or for not responding to an email message or even to a column like this one. But the world is the poorer for your not sharing your thoughts. We all need each other's contribution. Free spontaneous communication not only lubricates human relationships; it is vital to the proper development of ideas, concepts and plans.

Even when we make up our minds to confront, explain, speak out or write that response note, we have to remember what historian Henry Brooks Adams observed: "No one means all he says, and yet very few say all they mean, for words are slippery and thought is viscous." Even so, it is worth the risk.

I'll give the last word to philosopher and poet Johann Wolfgang von Goethe: "One ought, every day at least, to hear a little song, read a good poem, see a fine picture and, if it were possible, speak a few reasonable words."[3]

1. *Johnson's (Revised) Universal Cyclopaedia: A Scientific and Popular Treasury of Useful Knowledge* (New York: A.J. Johnson & Co, 1836), 686.

2. Henry Adams, *The Education of Henry Adams: An Autobiography* (Boston: Houghton Mifflin, 2000), 451.

3. Johann Wolfgang von Goethe, *Wilhelm Meister's Apprenticeship* (Whitefish, MT: Kessinger Publishing, 2004), 288.

⤞ COLUMN 32 ⤝
BUILDING MEMORIES

A few years ago we moved house…again. Usually a traumatic event. Helping us that morning was an assortment of neighbours, church friends and family, including our 12-year-old twin grandsons—the boys who made Jo and me grandparents. As they were carrying out the twin beds Tyler observed, "We were the first grandkids to sleep on these beds, and last night we were the last ones to sleep on them in this house."

Ryan said, "Grandma, I like this house. We had so much fun in it." True. They remember this place with pleasure. But wait a minute. What about all the nasty times? Like the time they got their fingers pinched in the backyard swings? Or when they scraped their legs falling out of the tree in the corner? Blood and tears dripped both times.

It reminded me of what Paul said to his church friends in Philippi: "I thank my God for every remembrance of you" (Phil. 1:3, author's paraphrase). Excuse me? Every remembrance? Wasn't Philippi the place where he got that skin-tearing, bloody lashing and spent the night in jail with his feet in the stocks? Yes, but that horror is not what he focused on. Paul remembered the jailer who washed his wounds while he listened to the Good News, and then became the first household to join the growing new church.

I learned two lessons from my grandsons that day. The first: We need to control our memories. We need to focus on the positive stuff in situations and in people. I carry thousands of memories of our decades with the Canela in Brazil. Let me assure you that many of them are not positive! Jo and I suffered in numerous ways— emotionally, physically, economically and socially. You name it, I can tell you a nasty story about it.

But I won't. Like my grandsons, I want to control what I remember. For instance, I don't want to remember the inconvenience of incessant traveling, but the churches I visit that are growing more excited about doing cross-cultural missions.

The second lesson from my grandsons is that we need to make it easy for other people to have good memories of us. The way we treat people builds memories of us for them. The couple we mentored to take over the Canela program once sent us a plaque with Paul's words on it: "We thank our God for every remembrance of you."

That plaque hangs in an honoured place. Over the past years, some people whom I recruited, mentored and supervised in Wycliffe have said words like this: "Thanks for getting me involved in this job. The past three years have been the best of my life."

They have good memories of us. What's more, I clearly remember every single one of those people, the exact words they said, the time and location they said it.

These lessons, learned from my young grandsons, apply universally. Not just between relatives and close friends, but between missionaries and church leaders. Between organizations' leaders. Between nationals and missionaries. Between trainers and trainees.

God designed human relationships to flourish in a positive atmosphere. Remembering the good stuff motivates us to thank other people. Most importantly, focusing on the positive things in our lives drives us to thank "God from Whom all blessings flow."

ADMINISTRATION AND QUALITY PRODUCTION

Missionary aviation mechanics are fanatics. They are intolerant, extreme, and I love it. Hey, my family and I flew over hundreds of miles of trackless jungle in those planes! It gave me great peace that the mechanics cut no corners. When, after a certain number of hours, an engine was due for an inspection, that plane was out of service, the engine inspected inside and outside, up and down, and every other way. I hope my doctor is as thorough when doing my annual physical checkup!

Those high aircraft maintenance standards were set by the manufacturer, the Brazilian government, and JAARS, Wycliffe's technical partner organization. The standards and procedures were all clearly stated in written policies. They were, no doubt, also fixed in the heads and hearts of the mechanics. But that was not all.

There was also an administrative structure in place to make sure the policies and procedures were adhered to. It reminds me of the administration adage, "What is INspected gets done, not what is EXpected." This is true in every human endeavour, even in missions, from servicing aircraft engines to producing Bible translations.

As Bible translators we were very much aware of Wycliffe's high standards for Bible translation. In accordance with the written policies, my wife and I needed to demonstrate certain levels of knowledge of the Bible, of linguistics, of culture, and of course, of proficiency in the language into which we were translating the Word. We also needed to demonstrate that the national translators with whom we worked were gifted in the use of their own language, that they knew how to think objectively about their language, and that they complemented my wife and me in the areas where we were weak—just as we complemented them.

Who made sure that all this was, in fact, the case? Well, my wife and I were highly motivated to produce the very best translation of which our team was capable. We had been well trained. And we were surrounded by a band of experienced consultants. This group of experts stood ready to help and advise in every aspect of our work: in linguistics, in cultural anthropology, in literacy, in translation, in Scripture use, etc.

But motivation, training and consultant resources were not enough to assure a high quality translation. There was also an administration that made sure the written standards, policies and procedures were being followed and the quality attained.

Unless a consultant checked out and approved a publication, it was not printed. Unless the translation passed all the tests, it never saw the light of day in print or audio. In the end, it was not the written policies that kept the production standard high. Nor was it our own fluctuating human motivation. Nor was it the training in workshops and seminars, nor the consultants' impassioned speeches on the importance of high standards. No, in the end it came down to capable, well-trained, authorized administrators doing their job.

Now, 15 years after we completed the translation program, some things have changed. The standards and policies are no longer in paper manuals, but on CDs where they are easily searched and read. Translators from a growing number of countries and a wide variety of cultures now bring their unique skills and backgrounds to the task. Many are mother-tongue translators, translating into their own language.

But other things have not changed. Translators are still motivated from within to do a good job. Consultants are still checking and preaching quality. And, all over the world, in every case where field leaders and their administrators "govern diligently" in the sense of Romans 12:8, quality standards continue to be met. Qualified administrators, both at home and on the field, are the key to quality missions work.

→ COLUMN 34 ←
MAKING DEATH A
HAPPY OCCASION

"We understand death for the first time when he puts his hand upon one whom we love." Millions of people agreed with eighteenth century writer Madame de Stael, when Death put his hand on Pope John Paul II in the spring of 2005.

This pope will be remembered, not only as the most traveled pope in all time, but as the one who displayed the least political correctness and the most internal consistency with basic Roman Catholic doctrine. His obituary, however, was not the only one the world read at that time.

The news media fully informed us of the last weeks of brain-damaged Terri Schiavo, who died after artificial feeding was stopped. That same weekend, noted Canadian conductor, composer and violinist Alexander Brott died at age 90. Quebec-born writer and Nobel laureate Saul Bellow passed away at age 89. The next day, Monaco's Prince Rainier III died.

These notable deaths, however, did not help me understand death better, nor did the deaths of the 2,500 Indonesian earthquake victims on Nias Island. It took the deaths of some people much closer to me to do that.

Ralph and Shirley were friends and financial partners in our Wycliffe ministries for many years. We strengthened our relationship as Ralph served on the Wycliffe Canada board when I was the CEO. Just a few months before the inoperable brain tumour appeared, he and Shirley took my wife and me out for dinner and a memorable symphony concert.

The tumour grew until the day Ralph went to be with his Lord on Easter weekend. All that time I kept thinking, "He is younger than I am—it could be happening to Jo and me."

Then, just a few days later, the brutal murders of Wycliffe translators Rick and Charlene Hicks shocked and saddened the whole Wycliffe family. Robbery appears to have been the motive that led to their murders and the burning of their home in Guyana, South America.

I met the Hickses in Surinam shortly after they were married. We talked about their ministry in their isolated location near the Wapishana village in Guyana. My first thought on hearing of their murders was, "Who is now going to help complete the Wapishana translation?" My second thought was, "For over 20 years my family and I lived and worked in very similar circumstances in neighbouring Brazil. This could have been us."

Through these deaths, I understand more clearly how important it is to live well in the present moment. I keep checking up on myself: Am I aware of God today? Do I see Him in the things that happen around me? Do I see Him in the people I meet? Am I showing my love for Him and for the people around me? Are my outer actions consistent with my inner beliefs?

Death may come through the hand of man, by accident, fatal illness or old age. How and when Death puts his hand on us is irrelevant. What matters is how we use the years God grants us.

Fifteenth century genius inventor and philosopher Leonardo da Vinci said it well: "As a well spent day brings happy sleep, so a life well used brings happy death."

→ COLUMN 35 ←
OIL DRUMS AND LINGUISTICS

Towing my suitcases behind me, I walked out of Trinidad's Piarco airport one February afternoon, right into a wall of sound. A steel band was welcoming me, and possibly several thousand other visitors, to the Carnival celebrations. For a week, right through to Ash Wednesday, calypso steel bands play nonstop for both enjoyment and competition in the capital city, Port of Spain.

What struck me again was the creativity of Caribbean peoples among whom we worked for three years. The steelpan, made from used oil drums, is the only acoustic musical instrument invented in the twentieth century—by Trinidadians. The steel orchestra is composed of instruments covering the full range of the conventional orchestra: the tenors, the double second, the guitars, the cellos, the quadro and six pan, the bass, plus the rhythm section. Steelpan music includes not only Afro-Caribbean music but extends to jazz, pop and classical with all the distinctive rhythms and tonality of the steelpan instrument. Nothing tops worshiping God listening to Handel's *Hallelujah Chorus* played on a dozen pans!

God made us to be creative. He is honoured and worshiped when we use our creativity to serve Him. We all have a deep-seated need to create, not noise, clamor and chaos, but music, order and pattern. This is obvious not only in music, but in language and linguistics.

In the early months of researching and learning the language spoken by the Canela people of Brazil, my wife and I charted a dozen vowel sounds on a phonetic chart. Later, when I showed it to our linguistic consultant, he frowned and said, "There is something wrong here. It looks ugly; it is not symmetrical. For instance, on the left corner of the chart you filled in a low, frontal, nasalized vowel, but on the right corner you have a blank. Go back to the village, listen again, and look for a low, back, nasalized vowel." We did go back, and we did find it, as well as other vowels to fit in the ugly holes in my chart. Linguistics is patterns, just like math. That's why one of Wycliffe's best language consultants had a Ph.D. in mathematics.

Genius mathematician and architect Buckminster Fuller used to say, "When I am working on a problem I never think about beauty. I only think about how to solve the problem. But when I have finished, if the solution is not beautiful, I know it is wrong." G. H. Hardy, another mathematician, said, "Beauty is the first test; there is no permanent place in the world for ugly mathematics." Nor for ugly linguistics.

As my wife and I searched for patterns and design in the seemingly confusing jumble of Canela language, we kept in mind Einstein's advice: "Make everything as simple as possible, but not simpler." The simplicity, elegance, symmetry and beauty in languages spoken by forgotten people groups are strong evidence for a Creative Designer God.

When, after many years, I had a whole sheaf of elegant, beautiful linguistic charts, I showed the patterns to one of our Canela language workers. He was surprised to see the designs in the language he had spoken all his life. I got the same stunned reaction from an atheist anthropology student when I showed her some of the intricate patterns of the Canela language. "How can these uneducated jungle people come up with such a beautiful language?" was her question.

How? For the same reason Trinidadians can produce such beautiful, intricate and heart-stirring music on an old oil drum. Just as God formed our DNA to create pattern, design and system, so He wants us to use the ability to discover patterns in all the languages of mankind—more than 6,500 beautiful and elegant languages! God has obviously greatly gifted Caribbean people with this ability to develop patterns and design. That is why I am so confident He will use many creative Caribbean people to go to the needy parts of Africa and Asia, to analyze languages, search for patterns, translate the Bible and transform societies.

Someday we will stand before the throne of God in heaven and sing in worship to Him in every language spoken on earth—possibly accompanied by a steelpan orchestra.

STEERING WHEEL OR SPARE TIRE?

I don't consider myself a prayer warrior, nor am I known as a man of prayer. That is not to say I don't believe in prayer, or that I don't pray. I do. I pray every day. I often write letters to God, highlighting specific requests and later thanking Him for positive answers. My 35 years of daily diaries contain frequent lines of prayer. I have preached and written about prayer, and God has used me to stimulate many other people to pray. Jo and I asked God to raise up a 30-person prayer team for us. He did. Thirty people have committed to pray for us and our ministry every day.

The year after we completed the Canela translation program I spoke to over 100 audiences. I gave them the opportunity to pray daily for a Canela man, woman or child by name and by picture. More than 400 people excitedly signed on. Now, 15 years later, I get notes from some of them saying, "I am still praying for my Canela boy, even though he is probably married by now and has a family of his own." Now those are people of prayer!

So if you asked me, "Jack, how is your prayer life? How much time do you spend on your knees?" the answers probably would not satisfy you. I would rather answer the question, "Jack, is God answering prayer in your life, your family and your ministry?" To that question I would say, "Yes, indeed He is!" and proceed to tell you stories of answered prayer. That is why I strongly believe in communicating with God, but as a writer, I practice prayer in my own way.

One time my wife Jo was preparing to do a personal, confidential interview with a young lady considering a career in Wycliffe. I happened to walk by the desk where she was studying the applicant's file and noticed she was crying. "Never walk away from a crying woman" is a principle I live by, so I stopped, put my hand on her shoulder and asked what was wrong. She quickly closed the confidential file and said, "I am going to interview a young woman, and I will need to discuss so many painful things."

On the spur of the moment, I said, "I will pray for you the whole time you are talking with her." Jo smiled, stood up, gave me a hug, said thanks and walked out the door with the file in her hand, leaving me standing there and saying to myself, "What have I done!? I have never prayed for any one thing for a solid hour in my life!"

So I sat down at my computer and started a letter: "Dear God, Jo has just left to talk with a young woman, and I have committed to pray for her for this hour..."

As I wrote, thoughts came into my head. I wrote, I thought, sometimes I cried. I wrote again, thought again, wrote some more. Suddenly I heard the door open. Jo was back. The hour was over, and I wasn't done praying yet! When I showed her what I had written, she looked at me with tears in her eyes and said, "This is exactly what we talked about, and the interview went very well."

Fellow Hollander Corrie ten Boom used to ask, "Is prayer your steering wheel or your spare tire?" It's a good caution against using prayer only in emergencies.

My advice is, hang onto the steering wheel of prayer in all situations, but do it in your own way, not in the way they teach you in books, or from the pulpit, or in columns like this one.

Find your own personal way to communicate with God.

TERRIBLE TUESDAY:
SEPT. 11 IN PERSPECTIVE

Most of us can remember the moment we first heard of the September 11 terrorist attack on New York in 2001. I was writing emails on my laptop in the living room of a Wycliffe friend in Curaçao when my hostess ran into the house shouting, "Er is iets vreselijks gebeurt in New York!" We clicked on the TV and, yes, something terrible was happening right in front of our eyes as we saw an airliner slam into the second World Trade Center tower. By the end of that day, 2,823 people died in the wreckage—a terrible Tuesday for New York, for the USA and for the world.

On that same terrible Tuesday 2,379 children died of malaria in Africa, the same number as had died on Monday, and would die on Wednesday, and the next day, for a total of one million African children dead from malaria in one year. On that same terrible Tuesday AIDS killed 6,300 Africans, and the next day, and the next for a total of 2,300,000 African people dead from AIDS that year. Elsewhere in the world on that same terrible Tuesday 35,000 people died of starvation—a one-day average of the 12,775,000 people killed by hunger in 2001.

What is so sad about these statistics is that deaths by malaria, AIDS and hunger are, for the most part, preventable—as are the deaths by murder of 15,000 people in North America alone, and the 42,000 deaths in automotive accidents that year. Altogether, around the world, about 56 million people died in 2001.

How many of those 56 million are now with the Lord? I can't help but wonder. What about the 56 million who are dying this year, and those who will die next year, and the next? How many of those will enter eternity to praise God? How many who will die have heard about the God Who made them and Who loves them? What am I doing this year, this week, today, to increase their chances to hear this Good News in their own language?

Oh, that 56 million a year would be added to the heavenly hosts to bring more glory and praise to our wonderful God! That's a goal worth living for—a goal worth dying for.

In the end, our life is not about us. It's not about people. It's not even about preventing untimely deaths. It is all about God. It is about what brings Him glory, about what makes Him famous, about what elevates Him in the eyes of every sentient being in the universe.

This focus on God is what makes working in cross-cultural mission agencies such as Wycliffe so exciting. Every day we get to do something toward bringing God's Good News to multimillions of people who, as yet, have no chance to hear it in the language they understand best. Every day we influence a person to get involved in this work as a volunteer, a financial partner, a member or a prayer warrior. Those that accept join in the excitement of helping people to connect with God.

There is no work on earth as foundational as preparing the Word of God in the heart language of people who have never had it. And God has granted us the privilege of being involved in some part of this task. Wow!

Preventing terrorist attacks, finding and implementing the cure for AIDS, or for cancer, for malaria or for world hunger are important. But let's face it, our bodies all will die someday. Yet Bible translation focuses on God Who loves every one on earth. Every body. Every mind. Every soul.

I can hardly wait to finish this column and get at it.

→ COLUMN 38 ←
THE PARABLE OF THE
USELESS SAMARITAN

"…and the Samaritan saw him and took pity on him. He knelt down beside him and said unto him, 'Oh, those robbers wounded thee terribly. If only I had some wine, I would cleanse thy cuts. If only I had some oil, I would soothe thy wounds. If only I had some clean cloths, I would bandage thee to stop the flow of thy blood. Would that I had a donkey, I would surely put thee thereon, and take thee to an inn and take care of thee. And if I had money I would pay the innkeeper to look after thee. But alas, I am poor and have nothing, so I must leave thee in thy misery beside the road and go on my way.'"[1]

I heard the basic principle again the other day from the flight attendant: "…and in the unlikely event of a sudden drop in cabin pressure, your oxygen mask will drop down from the ceiling. Those of you who have children, put on your own mask first before you help your child." Put on your own mask first. Wise words.

During our first term of service in Brazil, my wife and I were useless Samaritans. We staggered about wanting to help others while gasping for oxygen ourselves. That was in the days when we had more idealism than sense. We had about 40 percent of our financial support promised and blithely left for the field, where we immediately had to borrow money from other missionaries just to buy groceries. In the Canela village, surrounded by all sorts of human needs, we had barely enough diarrhoea medicine for our own kids, let alone for hundreds of suffering Canela children. We saw babies die from lack of 25 cents' worth of antibiotic. We even had to cut back our Canela language study because we couldn't afford the one dollar a day to pay our language worker. We felt useless and helpless.

In our first furlough back in Canada, we seriously set about building not only a prayer team, but a committed financial partnership team.

We compiled a huge mailing list, prayed a lot, wrote many letters, followed up contacts, visited people, phoned friends, cast vision for the Canela, gave people opportunity to commit to support our ministry. Then we returned to minister in Brazil with 100 percent of our support quota promised and coming in.

What a difference in our effectiveness! Instead of working with one language worker a few hours of each day, we worked with three or four full time, and sometimes up to a dozen part time. We bought crates of medicines, medical manuals, surgical and dental instruments, and taught some Canela men how to use them. We prayerfully used modern medicines to heal the sick. Our credibility and influence grew to the point where we were accepted as healers, as teachers, and eventually as messengers from God. The money our financial partners provided made the difference. Partners are clearly a critical and vital part of a missionary's ministry.

What is also clear is that even though the missionary is responsible to communicate his God-given vision for ministry to potential partners, it is God who builds the team.

A few years ago, a young missionary couple who needed their own financial partnership team asked me how many partners my wife and I had and where they came from. I told them we currently had 63. Then I did a quick check and generated the following list:

- Five since 1965, from the church we pastored before joining Wycliffe.

- One since 1966, from our sending church.

- Sixteen since 1966, from my wife's home church and personal friends. (See why I married her?)

- Ten since 1966, from Bible school friends.

- Three since 1966–1990, from short-term missionaries we met in Brazil.

- Five since 1966–2002, from immediate family and relatives.

- Five since 1966–2002, from my home church and personal friends.

- Five since 1971, from the church we attended during our first furlough.

- Three since 1982, from the church we attended during our third furlough.

- Two since 1994, from the church we attended after return from Brazil.

- Eight since 1992–1995, met during speaking trips.

Obviously God is not stuck in a box when He raises up a financial support team for His missionaries.

Wycliffe sending organizations around the world have now adopted the policy of members having 100 percent of financial support promised before taking on an assignment.

Good move. We all want to be good Samaritans, the kind with compassion in their hearts, knowledge in their heads and money in their hands.

1. See Luke 10:30–34 for the real story.

⊹ COLUMN 39 ⊰
MISSIONARIES HAVE BIGGER BRAINS

I have always suspected we multilingual, cross-cultural missionaries have bigger brains, but now there is scientific evidence. (No, I didn't say we have bigger heads, although some of us who are Dutch like I am, and gifted with a strong ego, have been described thus.)

I just read an article titled "Neurolinguistics: Structural Plasticity in the Bilingual Brain," in the journal *Nature*.[1] The researchers reported that people who speak two languages fluently have more grey matter in their left inferior parietal cortex, which, as you may remember from school, is the region of the brain responsible for language.

What's more, they found that the earlier people learned a second language, preferably before age 35, and the more fluent they were in it, the denser the grey matter.

The step to seeing how this applies to missionaries is a small one. The evidence for the study was collected in Europe with people fluent in both English and Italian: relatively closely related languages. Think how much stronger the evidence would be in the case of cross-cultural missions workers and linguist-translators in Africa or Asia where the languages differ totally from the missionaries' own language.

And that's not all. Most linguist-translators need to be more than just bilingual. For instance, after seven years in Brazil, I spoke four languages and could understand, at least partially, four more. This is not uncommon, especially among our African and Asian colleagues.

Sometimes I hear people refer to us foreign workers as our "wonderful missionaries" who have "sacrificed so much." I don't like being "pedestalized," but there is some truth to this. We do leave friends and relatives and home, and our financial situation is often precarious.

We usually respond, quoting Jesus, "No one who has left home or brothers or sisters or mother or father or children or fields for me and the gospel will fail to receive a hundred times as much...." (Mark 10:29–30).

Now it turns out Jesus was not just talking about receiving more brothers and sisters, etc., but bigger and better brains too.

Although the *Nature* article does not mention God, He is the One Who made our brains and bodies. Scientists guesstimate that packed inside the skull of every human being are 100 billion brain cells, each cell with the potential of making multiple connections capable of physically developing the brain. As we develop skills, speak and think, the relevant parts of our brains develop also. Our brains may grow even more cells, and certainly do grow more dendrite branches to increase the neural connections needed for learning.

King David wrote about this in Psalm 139:13–14: "You created my inmost being; you knit me together in my mother's womb. ...I am fearfully and wonderfully made." Though not a neuroscientist, David was right on. No wonder he praised God.

I wish that all 6.6 billion people on earth today would praise God for how wonderfully He has made them—and for how wonderfully He has provided the Way for them to be with Him forever! That's what God wants.

It will not happen, however, until all people have a chance to hear or read, in their own heart languages, that God loves them enough to send His Son to be their Saviour. The current plan is to have a Bible translation program started in every language of the world that needs it by the year 2025. By then the world population is expected to be 8.6 billion.

Cross-cultural missionaries, sent out by churches from almost every country in the world, continue to penetrate into thus-far-neglected cultures and subcultures to learn languages and bring the Good News. As a result, more and more people choose to connect with the God of the Bible and praise Him for Who He is and what He does.

Oh yes, the other result is that the missionaries' brains get bigger, but, in comparison, that's a relatively minor point.

1. A. Mechelli, J. T. Crinion, U. Noppeney, et al., "Neurolinguistics: Structural Plasticity in the Bilingual Brain," *Nature* 431, no. 7010 (2004): 757.

LONELY TEENAGE GIRL MEETS BEER-DRINKING BOY

Once upon a time, long, long ago, in a land far, far away, there was a lovely, though lonely, teenage girl. She lived and worked far from her home and family. Once, on her day off, she saw a tall, handsome teenage boy she liked. When the boy asked the girl to go for a bike ride with him, the girl said yes, because she was lonely, and the boy was attractive.

They biked and talked for a long time, much enjoying each other's company, until they came to a roadside café. The handsome boy invited the lovely girl to sit down at one of the little tables on the flagstone court and have a drink. She ordered lemonade, he ordered a beer. After they had sipped their drinks for a few minutes, the boy excused himself to visit the men's room. When he returned he found his beer glass empty.

"Where's my beer?" he asked, puzzled.

"Down there," she replied, pointing at the foamy wet flagstones beside the table.

During the conversation that followed they learned much about each other. He discovered that she did not intend to start a relationship with a young man who drank beer and she was willing to risk his friendship to preserve her well-thought-through standards. She discovered that he didn't really like beer, but thought he needed to show her that he was a man in accordance with the local saying, "Hij is geen man die niet drinken kan." (He is no man who cannot drink.)

That lonely girl with the high standards was my mom and the boy who wanted to prove his manhood was my dad. I first heard this story 40 years after I had my own similar experience of dating a girl with principles. She had heard of my reputation for flirting and kissing girls, so very early in our relationship she told me, "Don't kiss me on the lips unless you are ready to tell me you love me. And don't tell me you love me, unless you are ready to ask me to marry you."

After many enjoyable (though kiss-less) dates with this girl, one warm summer evening, sitting on a lakeshore after a sundown canoe ride, I leaned over and kissed her on the lips, then said, "I love you," and kissed her again, then said, "Will you marry me?" and kissed her again. She said, "Yes," and we continued to kiss. From first kiss to being engaged to be married took about 15 seconds. Neither of us has ever been sorry she shared her principles with me from the start.

For the last 15 years, whenever I have spoken to an audience of young people, I have never failed to say, "Set some life standards, and have a high goal, a great dream of what you want to be and do in your life. Then share that life goal with your friend on your first date. If you feel closer to your goal when you are with your friend, go ahead and have another date. If, however, your friend's response is negative, or you feel more distant from your goal, let that be your last date. You are better off without him or her."

The rest of us also need to set biblical goals to attain and principles to live by. Then each of us needs to ask himself or herself, "Am I willing to risk my career, my financial security, my human relationships and my personal comfort to stick to my principles and attain my goals?"

Hopefully we will answer, "Yes, I am!"

TWENTY-FOUR THINGS I HAVE LEARNED IN WYCLIFFE

Here are 24 things I have learned during my 444 months as a Wycliffe member:

1. A specific strategy, if practiced long enough, eventually becomes a core value.

2. There is no correlation between the amount of work accomplished and the amount of financial support received that month.

3. If God had wanted academics to have a vote, He would have given them the ability to make decisions. Instead, He gave them infinite capacity to gather facts and to discuss them.

4. The traditional monthly Day of Prayer always arrives unexpectedly.

5. No connection or relationship exists between the final amount stated in the official recommended support quota and the actual monthly support income.

6. Canadians get used to being taken for Americans. Eventually.

7. In a monolingual language-learning situation, the most eager teachers are teenage boys. Thus the first ten phrases learned can never be used in public.

8. The fewer clothes worn by a passenger in a JAARS missions plane, the higher (and colder) the altitude at which the plane is flown.

9. A direct one-to-one correlation exists between the need to make a long trip and the gastrointestinal distress of the traveler.

10. Snakes grow in length by 10 percent each time the story is told. On furlough they grow by 25 percent, unless a spouse is present to hear the story.

11. No matter what subject is brought up in a Wycliffe or SIL meeting, somebody will take it too seriously.

12. Never walk away from a crying spouse.

13. The ordinary working linguist rewrites linguistic papers to the point where he or she no longer fully understands them. That is when they are accepted for publication.

14. Each motorcycle rider is granted a certain number of accident-free miles. The motorcycle should be sold before that number is reached.

15. An efficient executive secretary triples the effectiveness of the administrator to whom he or she is assigned. In many cases the administrator becomes redundant.

16. Furloughs [n. a break from duty, a vacation] are not.

17. Do not confuse a Wycliffe career, even a career as a Bible translator, with life.

18. Hebrew and Greek are fascinating languages; so are 6,910 others.[1]

19. Never write linguistic data or drafts of translation on both sides of a piece of paper.

20. Technolust inflames 90 percent of male Bible translators and 10 percent of the female ones.

21. Living below your means lets you sleep well at night.

22. Never try to talk your way out of a situation you behaved your way into.

23. When traveling keep PTM (Passport, Ticket, Money) next to your skin at all times. Outside of North America and Western Europe, also carry TP.

24. Writing a column in which one of the readers' options is to laugh will offend some.

1. Wycliffe Bible Translators, Intl. annual statistics 2005 (Dallas, TX).

⟡ COLUMN 42 ⟡
GOD'S PLAN—OUR IMPROVEMENT

Not too long ago Jo and I were in Jamaica to promote Jamaicans doing cross-cultural missions work in Africa and Asia. Jamaica, by the way, claims to have more churches per square mile than any other country on earth. I believe it. Every possible denomination in North America came to Jamaica in the last couple of hundred years and planted churches carrying its own brand of Christianity. There are also a number of indigenous, homegrown varieties. It makes for an interesting mosaic. Although denominationalism is strong, there is the beginning of a trend to cooperate. The Jamaica Evangelical Association already has 20 denominations as members. What is even more interesting is that Jamaica sent out missionaries to Africa before Europe did—a great missions legacy.

During nine days I had 21 opportunities to publicly present the Church's responsibility to be active in missions, and the foundational part Bible translation plays in it. We presented a pastor's *Window on Wycliffe* informational workshop in three different locations. I spoke in three different churches on the first Sunday and enjoyed giving one television and two radio interviews. It was a great week, even though it was still short of John Wesley's norm of preaching three times a day.

A short Urbana video clip we show during the pastors' *Window on Wycliffe* makes a strong impact, especially when I follow it up with a chart of statistics.

I call it *God's Annual Financial Provision for World Evangelization.* Researchers estimate that the annual income of Christians around the world is US$12.3 trillion. Of that amount Christians give 1.7 percent to the Church to fund all Christian causes. Of the amount given, 94.6 percent is spent in the home country. Of the 5.4 percent that goes to foreign missions, only 1 percent goes to evangelize hidden people groups, including those who still do not have the Scriptures in their heart language.[1]

Boiling down these statistics to an understandable level, this is what you get: On the average, a Jamaican Christian earning an income of $12,300 keeps $12,090 and gives $209 to all Christian causes. Of this amount $197 is spent in the home country, while $11 goes to all foreign missions. Of this amount, 11 cents is spent on reaching the 10,000 traditionally overlooked people groups of which more than 2,500 do not yet have any part of the Bible in their heart language.[2] (Many Christians, of course, earn far more than $12,300 per year.) This is the current situation.

If, on the other hand, Christians budgeted in accordance with *God's Annual Financial Provision* based on the biblical tithe and a strategic 50/50 allocation of the funds, this is what you would get: A Christian earning an income of $12,300 would keep $11,070 and give $1,230 to all Christian causes. Half of this amount—that is, $615—would be spent in the home country, and the other half on all foreign missions. Half of this amount—that is, $307—would be spent on overlooked people groups.

The result would be that the home church budget would increase more than three times, from $197 to $615, to spend in the home country. Funding for total foreign missions would increase 55 times, from $11 to $615. And the amount spent on reaching minority language groups would increase an astronomical 2,790 times, from 11 cents to $307! This is God's plan. Unfortunately God's money managers—that is, Christians around the world—have "improved" on this plan to the point that mission agencies like Wycliffe have been trying to operate on 11 cents instead of on a major share of the $307.

Praying to God to supply the finances to complete the worldwide Bible translation task in this generation is akin to the early church praying for Peter's release from prison while he is outside pounding on the door. God has already amply supplied. Except for a number of blessed exceptions, statistics show the Church today to be as steeped in materialism as the Jews in Old Testament times were steeped in idolatry. Oh God, awaken the rest of Your Church!

1. Overlooked people groups speak minority languages and live in unique subcultures, often in out-of-the-way places.

2. Wycliffe Bible Translators, Intl. annual statistics 2005 (Dallas, TX).

TORONTO LAW PROFESSOR GIVES GOD A BREAK

The German university professor was impressed and appreciative. He was visiting the Canela village in Brazil to study some aspects of Canela culture, and we had become friends. He valued our linguistic research and was delighted to get a copy of our dictionary. One evening, toward the end of his stay, he asked about the kinds of problems and fears the Canela people had to deal with. My answer startled him. He looked up from his notepad and exclaimed, "But there are no ghosts!"

He then spoke passionately about needing to educate the Canela people to abandon old superstitions. He was emphatic about their need to deal with their fears of ghosts of the ancestors, malicious spirits and witchcraft by accepting that these things simply do not exist. He also urged me to help the Canelas to overcome these superstitions.

By this time I was grinning broadly and beginning to chuckle as I said, "Remember who you are talking to. I'm a Christian. I am a Bible translator. I believe in all these things. God is a Spirit. The Bible is full of narratives about spiritual beings, both good and bad. The whole point of our being here is to give the Canelas a choice to make a spiritual connection with their Creator God."

He looked at me open-mouthed. "But you are educated. How can you believe in God?" This led to a long conversation. Later that night he stood up to leave. As he shook hands in the German manner, he said, "Jack, in my life in Germany, and all my years as visiting professor in Brazilian universities, you are the first educated person I have ever met who really believes in God and the Bible."

I thought of this incident while reading the news about a long-delayed inquiry into the shooting of a First Nations man by police during a protest meeting some years ago. For two centuries Canada's aboriginal people have complained that the European settlers have not respected their burial grounds. "We don't disturb them [grave sites]," Native elder Clifford George explained. "It disturbs the soul. They become restless."

The best quote of all, however, was from a law professor at the University of Toronto who declared, "It's not just a physical world for aboriginal people. It's also a spiritual world."

Whew! At last a breakthrough! Now that this point has finally been established by a Toronto lawyer, hundreds of thousands of First Nations peoples in Canada can heave a deep sigh of relief. For them the struggle against government-sponsored secularism is over. Belief in spiritual realities is finally accepted as being part of the real world, not just something relegated to private meditations and quaint ceremonies. Hundreds of millions of other aboriginal peoples in countries around the world will also be able to take courage.

Okay, I admit it. I'm being sarcastic and a bit cynical. But what the professor said about it being "a spiritual world" is, of course, true.

Nearly 2 billion Christians around the world would agree. As would 1.2 billion Muslims, and 820 million Hindus, and 400 million Buddhists, and 20 million Sikhs, and 14 million Jews, etc.

Just because a few million influential Europeans and North Americans have accepted secular humanism as their religion, deleting God and anything spiritual from their minds, hearts and lives, does not mean that God does not exist.

He does exist, and not just scribbled in the margins of social, economic and political life. He is there, right in the middle of the page. He is in the whole book of human life. In fact, it is all about Him, because it is *also* a spiritual world. Always has been, always will be.

---

1. Gloria Galloway, "Ipperwash Inquiry Hears Native History," *Globe and Mail*, July 14, 2004.

"DULCE EST DESIPERE IN LOCO"

Time for a light column, and time for a chuckle or two.

The activities of the French and Quebec Language Police are always amusing—when observed from a distance. The law calls for everything to be in standard French, no change, and no mixture with other languages allowed. This includes advertising, even signs in the windows of stores. Only French allowed in offices and factories. Terms like *le weekend* are anathema. Now the Language Police are patrolling the information highway, chasing down non-French words on Internet websites of companies located in Quebec.

I am sure these French language purists know everything there is to know about the French language. But, unfortunately, there is a lot they don't know about the nature of language.

God's creation is filled with variety and diversity. This includes languages, which He created with the tendency to keep on changing and growing, much to the dismay of today's linguistic purists.

Ferdinand de Saussure (1857–1913), a French-speaking Swiss linguist, put it this way: "Time changes all things: there is no reason why language should escape this universal law."

He is not the only knowledgeable person to understand this. H. L. Mencken (1880–1956), writer, editor and critic, expanded the theme: "A living language is like a man suffering incessantly from small haemorrhages, and what it needs above all else is constant transactions of new blood from other tongues. The day the gates go up, that day it begins to die."

Ernest Weekley (1865–1954), lexicographer, agrees: "Stability in language is synonymous with rigor mortis."

Ralph Waldo Emerson once said, "Language is a city to the building of which every human being brought a stone."

In the same way that God created us all with different and unique personalities, the way we express ourselves is also unique and personal. Linguists call our individual language usage pattern an idiolect, from Greek *idio-* (personal, peculiar), and *dialect* (language unique to a group of people). Each of us has a unique way in which we put words together. That's our idiolect. No one else speaks it the way we do.

Some languages are dying out. Some simply disappear. Others, like ancient Latin, are no longer spoken as anyone's mother tongue, but remain useful for historical reasons, and because the body of literature yields a lot of neat quotes. For instance, Horace's advice to his translator is still pertinent: "Nec verbum verbo curabis reddere fidus interpres." (As a true translator you will take care not to translate word for word.)

I like to see ancient quotes converted to current use. Like Julius Caesar's quote after the battle of Zela: "Veni, vidi, vici." (I came, I saw, I conquered.)

I hope no missionary will ever refuse to let qualified nationals take over and say of himself, "Veni, vidi, velcro." (I came, I saw, I stuck around.)

Here's a useful one when watching TV or browsing the Internet: Caveat spectator. (Let the watcher beware.)

Nunc tutus exitus computarus. (It is now safe to turn off your computer.)

Purgamentum init, exit purgamentum. (Garbage in, garbage out.)

Writing this column gives me yet another outlet for my *insanabile cacoëthes scribendi* (a incurable passion to write).

The title of this column is my vacation motto: Dulce est desipere in loco. (It is sweet to relax at the proper time.)

And after vacation: Amoto quaeramus seria ludo. (Joking aside, let us turn to serious matters.)

THE BENEFITS TO A LOCAL CHURCH ACTIVE IN GLOBAL MISSIONS

When a local church recognizes the centrality of global missions in the church and fully commits itself to obey Christ's Great Commission to evangelize the world and disciple the nations, it puts itself into a place where God delights to bless it (Acts 1:8; Mark 16:15; Matt. 28:19; Jer. 7:23; Acts 5:32).

1. As the church sends its best people to minister overseas instead of in the local congregation, and sends a significant part of the total church income far away outside the local church, it exercises a strong faith in God, which He then is in a position to reward with strong spiritual blessings (Ex. 12:5; Mal. 1:8–14).

2. As the congregation provides funds for ministries far away, with no possibility of any direct benefit returning to the local church or its people, the givers are laying up treasures in heaven (Mark 10:21).

3. As they give to the poor—those in the most desperate straits—they do what Jesus commanded and practiced when He was on earth (John 13:29).

4. As they give away significant amounts of money for the benefit of others far away, they break the power money tends to have over them and are able to give cheerfully, with a deep and passionate joy (Luke 16:13; 2 Cor. 9:7).

5. As they hear or read firsthand stories of what is happening in the world from regions desperately in need of God's Word, they stop being introverted, shortsighted Christians, and become outward-looking, other-centred, world Christ followers (Phil. 2:4).

6. As they get personally involved in supporting global missions, they multiply their opportunities to exercise all their spiritual gifts: gifts of faith in prayer, of giving, of service, of celibacy, of martyrdom, of leadership, of administration, etc. (2 Tim. 1:6).

7. As church families extend hospitality to missionaries by having them over for dinner, or to stay with them, they broaden their children's mental and spiritual horizons (Phil. 2:4).

8. As parents in the church demonstrate sacrificial giving, they help prevent the power of money from getting a foothold in their children's lives (Luke 18:22).

9. As parents demonstrate and teach biblically proportional giving to meet needs outside the family, outside the local church and outside the local community, they train their children to love our missionary God, not to love money (1 Tim. 3:3).

10. As church people learn more about the desperate conditions in which billions of people live in Africa and Asia, they become exceedingly thankful for their own lives and circumstances (Ps. 16:6).

11. As they practice strategic global missions involvement, they have the joy of knowing they are filling the deepest holes of need, caring for the most needy, reaching to the least-reached places in the world to practice ministry and exercise gifts (Luke 15:4).

12. As they pray for lost, hidden people groups in hundreds of countries around the world, they not only educate themselves in ways the ordinary Christian knows nothing about; they also know that they are exercising strong power in the spiritual war against Satan (Mark 11:24; 2 Cor. 10:4).

13. As the church makes sacrifices, the church grows both in size and in spiritual health to such an extent it is noticeable both in the community and in the rest of the denomination (Mal. 3:10).

As Christians from missions-active churches stand before the Lamb on His throne, praising Him alongside numberless millions of redeemed from every tribe and language and people group, they will thank God for the privilege of being used by Him to help translate His Word into every language on earth.

His "Well done, you good and faithful servants, enter into the joy of your Lord," will echo in their ears forever (Matt. 25:21; Rev. 7:9–10).

LEAVING ALL TO FOLLOW HIM

One of our missionary friends sat down to rest on his suitcase, looked at the stack of drums, crates, boxes and bags of stuff he was shipping to Brazil, and with a touch of irony quoted Peter's comment to Jesus: "Behold, we have left all to follow Thee."

Jo and I have lived for a significant length of time in at least 37 houses since our marriage in 1962. And we moved between some of those houses dozens of times. We learned to follow the rule "Less is better." Living full time in a 28-foot motor home for two years after we returned from Brazil helped us refine this rule. When we are preparing to move or travel, the back bedroom is usually the packing and shipping warehouse. Four large suitcases and several carry-on cases sit ready to be packed in priority according to the Next Trip packing list:

1. Tickets, passport, money.

2. Bible, speech notes.

3. Computer, peripherals and books.

4. Wycliffe brochures, books and videos.

5. Underwear, socks, shirts and pants.

6. More brochures, books and videos as space and weight permit.

Missionaries tend to struggle with the temptation to pack and haul personal goodies out to "the field." Of course, often it is simply good economic sense to bring things we already own or can transport cheaply to our field of service. We also need to bring along things we require for our life and work but simply cannot get on the field—like English language books for our kids and ourselves.

On the other hand, sometimes all this packing and hauling is just an attempt to make us feel comfortable, surrounded by the familiar things from home. We Westerners, with a strong streak of materialism in our cultures, are particularly prone to value material goods. We need to be careful of our relationship with our stuff.

Famous architect Frank Lloyd Wright once said, "Many wealthy people are little more than janitors of their possessions." May that never be said of us who claim to be followers of the One Who said He had nowhere to lay His head.

It's not just material things we need to leave behind when we follow Jesus. It is familiar faces, comfortable situations, cherished friendships and loved ones of every size and age. I am here to tell you that the older you get, the more difficult this part becomes. Jo and I honour our parents each time we remember the day we left for Brazil. We boarded the plane with our parents' three preschool granddaughters— their only ones. It's not just missionaries who make sacrifices; parents and grandparents also pay a price. Serving the homeless One means sacrifice of things we use and people we love.

That's why it's comforting to read in the same passage in Mark 10 a strongly stated promise of both present and future reward. Just think, for every brother, sister, mother, father or child left behind when we set out to follow Jesus, we will receive one hundred more. Homes and fields also.

And eternal life to boot. Wow!

GOD DESERVES MORE

In many of today's evangelical churches, worship equals music and music equals singing choruses. This is like sitting down with friends at a beautifully decorated Thanksgiving dinner table and being served only a cold hot dog. God deserves more than that.

The first mention of worship in the Bible had nothing to do with music or singing. It was about a man who took his son out into the bush, tied him up, and prepared to slit his throat and burn his corpse. In Genesis 22:5 Abraham referred to this act of obedience as *worship*.

Other Biblical examples of worship certainly do involve music. Not only did the temple have professional musicians, but singers preceded an army into battle on at least one notable occasion. The great worship scenes described in Revelation all include loud singing as a form of worship.

Biblical worship, however, is much, much more than music. It also includes: offering sacrifices; kneeling down to pray; thanking God for Who He is and what He does; looking after widows and orphans; and giving to the poor. All these are acts of worship that please God, yet without any mention of music.

Where, for instance, is the reverent, worshipful public reading of full passages of the Word of God? I need to go to an Anglican church for that worship experience.

What about worshiping through the giving of tithes and sacrificial offerings? According to Urbana researchers, Christians around the world give only 1.7 percent of their income to church and other Christian ministries.[1] North American churchgoers give only slightly more. I wonder what God thinks of churches that resound with long, loud, teary-eyed, hand-clapping and foot-stomping worship singing while the enthusiastic singers give far below His 10 percent minimum standard established in the Old Testament. Does He feel like He has been called for dinner and just handed a pickle?

The white churches of South Africa under apartheid and the white churches of segregationist southern USA reverberated with loud, exuberant hymn singing. But where was the social justice?

Richard Foster's book *Streams of Living Water* lists six traditional ways of relating to God in worship.[2] I am most familiar with what Foster calls the Evangelical worship tradition: worship through living a Bible-centred life. Examples are Martin Luther, William Carey, C. S. Lewis and Billy Graham. Here are the other five:

- The Charismatic tradition: worship through living a Spirit-empowered life. Think of the Franciscans and the Pentecostal movement.

- The Holiness tradition: worship through living a virtuous life. The Puritans, John Wesley and Dietrich Bonhoeffer are examples.

- The Incarnational tradition: the sacramental life offering excellence in work as a form of worship. Michelangelo, Rembrandt, Milton, Bach, Handel and the Russian novelists come to mind.

- The Social Justice tradition: worship through living a compassionate life. The abolition of slavery movement, the Salvation Army, Florence Nightingale and Mother Teresa are examples.

- The Contemplative tradition: worship through a prayer-filled life. The Desert Fathers, Frank Laubach and Henri Nouwen model this tradition.

No doubt some Christians in evangelical congregations personally practice a number of these ways to worship, often aided by a strong liturgical church service. That still is not enough.

Evangelical churches need to come to grips with the fact that worship is not just music. God made us all uniquely able to express our love, devotion and worship in different ways. Churches must not narrow down their worship to one single method.

When we worship God with our lives, our giving, our work, our prayers and our compassion, as well as our music, it is like having a Thanksgiving meal of turkey with all the trimmings. God deserves no less.

1. *The Church Around the World; Lost People; Poverty,* videos (Madison, WI: InterVarsity/Urbana 2000).

2. Richard J. Foster, *Streams of Living Water: Celebrating the Great Traditions of Christian Faith* (San Francisco: HarperSanFrancisco, 1998).

IS GOD GETTING ANGRY YET?

The fighting and killing in the Middle East is not of recent origin. Reading in Isaiah, I was struck with the horrible descriptions of war: mass slaughter of civilian populations, sudden destruction, burning cities, widespread suffering and death, then slavery in exile. Why? What had ancient Israel done to provoke such anger, such horrific punishment?

Maybe the question should be, What had they *not* done? God wanted Abraham's descendants through Israel to be a God-led, God-exemplifying nation—one that would bring blessing to all the families of the earth. He wanted Israel to be high above all nations, a holy people, declaring His glory among all nations. He wanted all nations to recognize that God was the source of blessing on the land and its people, and that God's temple was a house of prayer for all nations. But they had not fulfilled God's plan for them.

Israel frustrated the missionary purposes of our missionary God. Their constant disobedience and continued selfish living, even as they kept up the outward forms of the temple sacrifices, brought shame on God. God's name was blasphemed among the nations because of Israel: the exact opposite of what God had intended. Instead of showing God's holiness to the nations, they profaned His holy Name among the nations. No wonder God was angry!

The only way God could get any glory from Israel was to publicly punish them in the presence of the very nations they should have been bringing to Him. In short, God designed Israel to be a missionary nation to spread the knowledge of God to all peoples. When they failed to bring glory to Him that way, He brought glory to Himself through His punishment of them.

Focus on these basic facts: God still wants the nations of the earth to know Him, to love Him, and to give Him glory. Christians are the spiritual descendants of Abraham. God's promise to Abraham that all the nations of the world were to be blessed by his descendants is, therefore, to be fulfilled in us. The Church around the world is God's chosen instrument to make this happen. Christian churches in every nation, therefore, are responsible to cross over into other cultures to reach all the peoples of the world with God's message of love.

Has this happened over the past 2,000 years? Well, sort of. The message of love has been spreading. The Church is growing. But at least two billion people still know nothing about God's love for them and His plan of salvation through Jesus Christ. Over a billion adults have never had the chance to learn to read—in any language. Hundreds of millions of hidden peoples are still trapped in illiteracy and ignorance, even though some of the Bible may be translated in a language they understand. And 270 million of them, speaking over 2,500 languages, still do not have a single word of Scripture translated into their language.[1]

So what is the Church doing about fulfilling God's ordained missionary purpose? Researchers estimate that only one person out of 22,000 Christians worldwide becomes a missionary to the marginalized and overlooked peoples of the world—the groups in the deepest spiritual need. They further estimate that on the average, worldwide, out of every $10,000 that they earn, Christians give only $170 to church and missions. Of that, $160 is spent right in the congregation that gave it, to pay for pastors' salaries, building maintenance, church programs and local evangelism. About $10 is spent on general foreign missions, mostly in countries that have already been reached with the gospel. Of that $10, only about 10 cents is spent on cross-cultural missions to the hundreds of millions of overlooked peoples, including those who still do not have even one verse of Scripture in their heart language.[2]

Is history repeating itself? First, God designed Israel to be a missionary nation to bring glory to His Name. They dishonoured God's Name by not doing their missionary job and He punished them. Next, God designed the Church to be a missionary force to bring glory to His Name. Is the Church dishonouring God's Name?

Pollster George Barna published a survey with the results of a question asked of people who said they were not Christians: "Is your impression of people in this group generally favourable?" Pastors and individual born again Christians ranked second and third on a list of eleven types of people. Evangelicals as a group, however, ranked tenth, below lesbians and just above prostitutes. (Military officers were ranked first.)[3]

What does that say about the reputation of the organized evangelical church among non-Christians? Is God's Holy Name not profaned when His people turn their backs on their calling? When churches focus on their own needs and wants? When they give only 1.7 percent of their income to God's work? When they spend only about 10 cents out of every $10,000 to spread the gospel to the lost and overlooked minority peoples of the world?

This kind of behaviour by His people used to make God angry.

1. Wycliffe Bible Translators, Intl. annual statistics 2005 (Dallas, TX).

2. *The Church Around the World; Lost People; Poverty,* videos (Madison, WI: InterVarsity/Urbana 2000).

3. Bible Network News Staff, with notes from Barna Research Group, "Evangelicals Less Favourable Than Lawyers, Lesbians—US Poll Reveals," *Bible Network News* (January 2003).

SHRUNKEN WORLDS: SHRUNKEN MINDS

Pain, if great enough, will shrink your world. For most of this week my world shrunk to my bed, my bathroom and me. No room for home and garden, or for relationships and conversation. No room even for my beloved laptop—full proof I was in a bad way. It has been a long time since I felt this way, probably not since the regular rainy season bouts of amoebic dysentery in the Canela village in Brazil (but this time without the fever, and without, thus far, discovered cause).

But pain is not the only thing that will constrict our worlds. Just check out two teenagers in love. You will soon realize nothing matters to them but each other. Not their schoolwork, nor their relationships with parents and siblings. Not even their after-school jobs matter. At least that is the impression I got a few weeks ago while paying for a purchase at a corner grocery. The checkout clerk talked steadily with her boyfriend on her cell phone, while ringing up sale after sale and handing back change to a whole file of customers, without once making eye contact with us—her world reduced by teenage love.

Some career-driven people live in a shrunken world: a world containing their career, their job relationships and their job skills, with barely enough room for family. Taking the reasons for divorce as evidence, the shrunken worlds of people climbing the corporate ladder, along with those driven by greed for money, often have no room for a spouse.

Yet something else concerns me even more. Ordinary, regular Christian people live in constricted worlds—worlds without room for many things that God intends us to include in our world.

Look at the content of the programs listed in the average church bulletin. How many of these programs focus merely on the here and now needs of the church people? Marriage and family, dieting and exercise, budgeting and money management. All these are important subjects that ought to have a place in a Christian's life, but they are also self-focused. Where is the wider world of service to those outside the church? Where is the expansive world of cross-cultural global missions?

Seminaries and Bible schools all over the Western world continue to produce graduates who know little about cross-cultural global missions. In some theological schools, it is possible to graduate without ever taking a single missions course. Some institutions do not even offer a missions course. No wonder then that some pastors live in a shrunken world confined to the here and now situation of their congregation. It is no surprise that their church pews are filled with people whose world horizons stop short of the plight of multi-millions of people all over Africa and Asia who have never heard of Jesus.

What is the remedy? How do we stretch our personal shrunken world? Jesus has the answer to the problem. The world of His disciples had diminished to themselves and their next meal. Jesus' solution: "Lift up your eyes, and look on the fields; for they are white already to harvest" (John 4:35, KJV). Or, as a modern version has it, "Open your eyes, and take a good look" (The Message).

A Christian businessman normally gave about $10,000 to various missions projects he heard about. Then one day he personally visited an overseas project in Africa. His eyes were opened, his horizons expanded, his world widened, and he gave half a million dollars to the ministry he had visited

Congregations with forward-looking elders send their pastors on a furlough to Africa or some part of Asia. As these pastors see the spiritual needs firsthand, their shrunken worlds expand and they return with a mission to expand the worlds of their congregations.

When my wife Jo and I checked out mission organizations 40 years ago, often the first question on the application form was, "How much pastoral or other home ministry work have you done? If none, do a couple of years before you apply."

I wonder what would happen today if churches would ask pastoral candidates, "How much global missions experience do you have? If none, do a couple of years before you apply."

Sounds like an effective world-expanding policy to me.

→ Column 50 ←
The Shortest, the Middlest, and the Longest

Psalm 119 is the longest chapter in the Bible. We all know that. Most of us know the shortest chapter is Psalm 117. But did you know that Psalm 118, the chapter in between the shortest and the longest, is the central chapter of the Bible? Yes, there are 594 chapters before it, and 594 chapters after it. I am not saying that the arranging of Bible books into their current order and the division into chapters and verses is inspired, but it does make for an interesting illustration about Christian centrality.

The "middlest" chapter, Psalm 118, is rich in worship themes and imagery. Right in the middle of this psalm is the well-known worship testimonial exalting God's Name: "The Lord is my strength and my song; he has become my salvation."

Churches around the world focus on this central theme of Scripture, found in the centre of the central chapter. And that is as it should be. Exalting the Name of God in worship should be central in our churches, in our homes and in our lives.

But this central chapter on worship is flanked by two notable psalms. Psalm 119 is not only the longest; it is also the psalm in which every verse speaks of God's Word, all 176 of them. And Psalm 117 speaks of worldwide missions: "Praise the Lord, all you nations; extol Him, all you peoples."

How appropriate that the three chapters in the centre of the Bible should focus on cross-cultural missions, God-honouring worship and the life-changing Word of God!

"You have exalted above all things your name and your word" (Ps. 138:2). The inspired psalmist reveals the two things God holds in highest esteem: His glorious Name and His Word. We focus on these through worshiping His Name with a fervent heart and meditating on His Word with an obedient heart.

So how does missions relate to these two? Very simple. Missions is penetrating cultures with the Word of God in the language of the people, so that the Holy Spirit can bring them into a saving relationship with God, turning them into worshipers, exalting the Name of God and being discipled through obedience to the Scripture.

As a young pastor I once asked a visiting missionary speaker what Scripture passage he would like to have read during the Scripture reading part of the Sunday morning service. His reply impressed me: "It doesn't matter what passage you read; the entire Bible is about missions." Over 40 years later, I can testify that, in a broad sense, missions is a theme that runs from early Genesis to late Revelation. No wonder missions comes into strong focus in one of the three central chapters!

Missions, worship and the Word are at the physical centre of our Bible. They should be central in our lives, central in our homes and central in our churches. Are they? Many of our churches focus hard on worship, but tend to neglect in-depth teaching of the Word, resulting in little motivation to be involved in cross-cultural missions.

Pastor John Piper keeps saying, "Missions exists because worship doesn't."[1]

Not yet. Not everywhere. Not among those people groups who do not yet have God's Word in their language.

1. John Piper, *Don't Waste Your Life* (Wheaton, IL: Crossway Books, 2003), 162.

THAT CHRISTMAS STAR

Just what kind of starry sign in the night sky brought those astrologers west to Bethlehem? A couple of stubborn facts stand in the way of a clear answer.

First, no one knows just what those mystics from the Parthian empire saw. Two thousand years ago, people seeing any heavenly object bright enough to attract attention were apt to call it a "star." Meteors, for instance, were "falling" stars; comets were "hairy" stars; novae were "new" stars and planets were "wandering" stars.

Secondly, no one knows in what year Jesus was born. Calendars were recalculated several times and some mistakes were made. The guess is around 3 or 4 BC. What is more sure is that He was born in the spring, not in midwinter. Shepherds of Palestine stayed with their flocks during the night to help deliver the lambs that were born during the spring.

But, fascinated by the possibility of pinpointing both that mysterious heavenly sign and the date of the birth of Christ, astronomers have been running their planetariums backward to about 2,000 years ago. Here are the results of their calculations.[1] Take your pick.

- A conjunction of the planet Jupiter (the king planet) with the star Regulus (the king star) not once but, through Jupiter's retrograde motion, three times around 3 BC.

- Nine months later, Jupiter had such a close conjunction with the planet Venus that they could not be separated by the naked eye. Other than the moon, it would have been the absolute brightest object in the night sky.

- Jupiter and Saturn had a conjunction in 7 BC.

- Jupiter, Saturn and Mars had a notable triple conjunction

in 6 BC.

- The planet Uranus, until then unknown, may have been discovered.

- A supernova explosion of a star in Capricorn, noted by the Chinese in 4 BC.

- An unknown major comet (but not Halley's, which came by too early) in 12 BC.

- A combination of any number of the above.

There is no satisfactory conclusion. But, now that we are thinking about stars, let's check out an astonishing multi-star project the Hubble Space Telescope completed recently—one that would have blown those wise men right off their camels. Hubble focused its lens on a tiny empty-looking section of sky about one-tenth the size of the diameter of a full moon. After staring at this spot for a week and a half it processed about 10,000 galaxies. Not individual stars, but 10,000 galaxies like our own Milky Way galaxy, which is estimated to contain between 100 billion to 1 trillion stars!

If astronomers repeated this experiment on another tiny section of sky, would they find another 10,000 galaxies? Probably. If they repeated the experiment 12.7 million times, they would have a picture of the total sky, and 13 billion years of cosmic history. How many stars would they find? The number would be a 1 with 22 zeros. Or maybe 23 zeros or 24. Who knows? Who cares?

Well, I care. Not about how many gazillions of stars God made. I care about the fact that He did make them, and that He reveals His creative power to astronomers today. I care even more about the fact that this incredibly powerful Creator loved the people of tiny little planet Earth enough to send His own Son as a Baby to grow and live and die and come alive again so that we might know that great Creator God. And I care that He reveals Himself, His character, His holiness and His love through His Word.

I also care about the fact that after 2,000 years, millions of Iraqis and Iranians, descendants of those ancient Parthian mystics, still don't know about that Baby who came from outer space to save them.

But for me, the most emotional number at Christmas time is 2,500.[2] It has nothing to do with how many stars there are in the universe, but it brings tears to my eyes. This number, 2,500, is the approximate number of language groups that still do not have even one verse of the Great Creator's Word translated into their mother tongue.[2]

But there is hope. Thousands of missions-minded people from all over the world are getting involved in Bible translation The number of African, Asian and South American missionaries and volunteers working at this task will soon outnumber the missionaries from northern countries.

All these missionaries leave home, not to follow a starry sign, but to follow the One whose birth the star from the east announced.

1. The astronomical information was compiled from the following journals: *The Quarterly Journal of the Royal Astronomical Society*, vols. 18, 19, 20; *Astronomy Quarterly*, vol. 3; *The Griffith Observer*, Dec. 1980; *Sky and Telescope*, vol. 36.

1. Wycliffe Bible Translators, Intl. annual statistics 2005 (Dallas, TX).

→ COLUMN 52 ←
THE THIRD INCARNATION

During Christmas week we celebrate the Word of God becoming human flesh in the person of Jesus Christ—the First Incarnation. Yes, the first of three incarnations. No, this is not heresy.

In the First Incarnation, God revealed Himself to this world by becoming a perfect human being—a love-motivated miracle that solved mankind's greatest problem. Now, through Christ's life, death and resurrection, we have access to God. All other problems now become relatively insignificant. In the light of our expectation of eternal life, none of earth's anxieties need to cause us distress. We are in the hands of the Father who loved mankind enough to send His own Son to die for us.

Looking back to the distant past we see a great cause to celebrate!

Christmas week is also a good week to celebrate the Second Incarnation—God revealing Himself through the lives of hundreds of millions of imperfect human believers all over the world. Christians everywhere, their human bodies the temples of the Holy Spirit, are the eyes, ears, mouth, hands and feet of Jesus. He goes only where we go. He does only what we do. He says only what we say. His Holy Spirit living in His people in every nation on earth draws tens of thousands of people to Himself every day. God reveals Himself and works in this world through human beings, grouped together in human organizations—local churches.

Looking all around the world we see the ongoing miracle of the Second Incarnation, another great cause for celebration!

Then, of course, Christmas week is also a good week to celebrate the Third Incarnation—God revealing Himself through the translation of His Word into thousands of human languages all over the world. No human language is incapable of revealing God to searching mankind. No human language is the only one capable of revealing God.

That's why Bible translation is the most foundational work in which any missionary, volunteer or supporter can be involved. God reveals Himself to thousands of people groups all over the world as His Word is translated in their own languages.

Looking two or three decades into the future we see the coming miracle of the complete fulfillment of the Third Incarnation—God revealing Himself in every single human language spoken on earth. It's another cause we can celebrate right now!

May God bless you as you celebrate His three Incarnations.

About Jack Popjes

Born in Holland, Jack immigrated with his family to Canada in 1950. He attended Berean Bible College in Calgary. Jack and Jo were married in 1962 and pastored a Baptist church in Innisfail, Alberta, for three years before joining Wycliffe in 1965. They left for Brazil in 1966 with three preschool daughters and began work with the Canela people in 1968.

When the Popjeses began their work, the Canela people were illiterate and there were no Christian believers. By the time the Scriptures in the Canela language were dedicated in 1990, there were many Canela believers, all able to read the Bible and teach others to read and obey the Word.

After the Popjeses left Brazil in 1990, they served with Wycliffe Canada and spoke at many conferences and banquets.

Jack served as CEO for Wycliffe Canada for six years, beginning in 1994. He led the organization through many changes in preparation for service in the new millennium. Jack was then appointed CEO of Wycliffe Caribbean with a mandate to restructure the organization, and find and train a successor. He completed this task in May 2004.

Currently Jack is the Wycliffe Canada national representative, serving as a speaker and writer.

CONTACT

You may contact the author utilizing the following methods:

Email: jack_popjes@wycliffe.ca
Paper mail: Box 85, Suite 1, RR 1, Onoway, AB, T0E 1V0 Canada

To receive the weekly *Look* column via email, send a blank email to Look-on@lists.wycliffe.org

Check the Wycliffe Canada website (www.wycliffe.ca) for archived articles, speaking calendar and more information about the author and his family.

To order additional copies of this book contact the Wycliffe Media Resource Center by calling 1-800-WYCLIFFE or email mrco@ wycliffe.org to place your order.